[1001] photos
Wonders of the World

© 2007 Copyright SA, France
© 2008 Rebo International b.v., Lisse, Netherlands

Text: Claire Lemoine
Editorial coordination: Isabelle Raimond
Photographic design: Frédéric Bar
Typesetting: A. R. Garamond, Prague, Czech Republic
Translated by Ian West in association with First Edition Translations Ltd.,
Cambridge, UK
Edited by First Edition Translations Ltd., Cambridge, UK
Copy editor: Erin Ferretti Slattery

ISBN 978 90 366 2411 4

Wonders of the World
[1001] photos

REBO
PUBLISHERS

Contents

Wonders of Nature

Wonderful Buried Treasures

Wonders of Sacred Art

Wonderful Cities

Wonderful Cultural Landscapes

Introduction

"Nothing can equal the power of man's love for his land, its forests, its rivers, its mountains, its rocks, its trees, its birds, its stones."

Jean-Marie Adiaffi, *La Carte d'identité*

Just over two thousand years ago, ancient authors listed Seven Wonders of the World as the most remarkable artistic achievements of their times—the Pyramids of Egypt, the Hanging Gardens of Babylon, the Statue of Zeus at Olympia, the Colossus of Rhodes, the Temple of Artemis at Ephesus, the Mausoleum of Halicarnassus, and the Lighthouse of Alexandria. Of the originals, only the pyramids survive; yet contemporary civilization has selected many, many more wonders, the heritage of all mankind.

The number of World Heritage sites recognized by UNESCO now stands at no less than 830, all of which demand preservation for their exceptional cultural value. The list has grown longer each year, since its inception in 1978. During its thirtieth session, in July 2006, the World Heritage Committee noted precisely 644 cultural sites, 162 natural, and 24 "mixed" locations spread around 138 countries—31 were classified as definitely endangered, being in a

6

pitiable state from the effects of time, natural catastrophes, or senseless vandalism.

The idea of an international movement charged with protecting our heritage was first mooted at the end of World War I. The planned flooding of the Nubian temples in Egypt during the construction of the Aswan Dam on the Nile, however, unleashed a real cultural revolution. UNESCO's appeal resulted in some 50 nations uniting to save the temples of Abu Simbel and Phile, which were dismantled and reconstructed from 1960. Other rescue campaigns followed— Venice, Italy; Mohenjo-Daro, Pakistan; Borobudur, Indonesia—leading in 1972 to the adoption of the Convention Concerning the Protection of World Natural and Cultural Heritage. Twenty years later, safeguards were extended to "cultural landscapes" and, from 2003, have included the preservation of "intangible cultural patrimony," i.e., oral heritage and traditional cultures. As a result, the list of heritage sites, still biased toward essentially European masterpieces, is gradually incorporating a more representative selection of the huge diversity of cultures and natural sites.

It is time now, however, to enjoy the wonders that that will open our eyes to the true value of humanity and planet Earth.

Wonders
of Nature

The surface of our blue planet is 70 percent water. Seas and oceans form extraordinary landscapes, islands, and shorelines famed not just for their outstanding natural beauty but also for their immense scientific interest.

Islands and coasts display an extreme and complex diversity that greatly enriches Planet Earth. Whether lying in polar, tropical, or temperate regions, deserts or barren wastes, they are vast natural laboratories for the observation of flora, fauna, ecosystems, and geological formations. Some sites on the World Heritage list cover scarcely three or four square miles; others extend over many thousands. Each one, from atoll or sand island to coastal mountain range, is unique and remarkable. Together, they teach us about the history of the earth, changing geological formations, and biological evolution.

Unsurprisingly, such a variety of environments favors the development of countless types of animal and plant, which are often rare or endemic to a single locality. Occasionally, they even contribute to the evolution of species. The protection of a certain number of habitats or reserves for flora and fauna—as well as the great migration highways of the ocean depths—is aimed at the preservation of this incalculable biodiversity.

The fascination of peoples with their surroundings frequently adds a strong "intangible" value to the treasure entrusted

Where Land Meets Sea

to their safekeeping. In the Pacific, for instance, the Hawaiian Islands have their Polynesian goddess, Pele; off the Antrim coast, in the North Channel that connects with the Atlantic, Giant's Causeway, with its 40,000 basalt pillars, has won a place in Irish folklore.

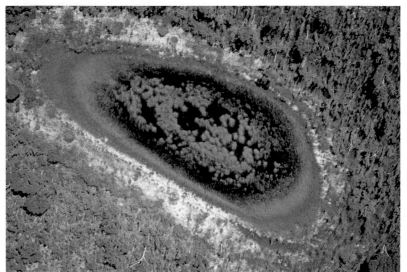

Fraser Island, off Queensland, Australia, in the Pacific—the world's largest sand island. In addition to its dunes and multicolored sand cliffs, it boasts half the planet's "perched" dune lakes, as well as majestic remnants of humid rainforest.

The Pitons, Santa Lucia, Caribbean Sea/Atlantic Ocean.
The volcanic islands conceal dozens of plant and bird species in a belt of humid tropical forest. Its coral reefs provide habitats for a wide spectrum of creatures, while turtles come to reproduce on the beaches.

13

The Great Barrier Reef, in the Coral Sea, off Queensland, Australia. Some 1,625 miles (2,600 km) long, the world's largest coral reef consists of more than 2,000 islands and 3,000 reefs, including the spectacular Heart Reef (right-hand page). It is home to thousands of species of coral, fish, and mollusks.

The Belize Barrier Reef, in the Caribbean, the largest barrier-reef in the northern hemisphere.

This unusual natural system shelters endangered species like the sea tortolse, the manatee, and the American saltwater crocodile.

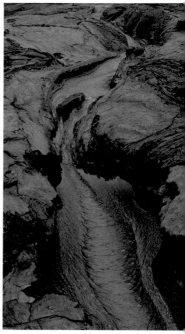

Kilauea, Hawaii, United States (Pacific Ocean).
With Mauna Loa, which towers 13,680 ft. (4,170 m) above Hawaii, it is one of the world's most active volcanoes. The area is of immense geological interest and contains many rare birds, a unique fauna, and forests of giant ferns.

[1] Coastline of the Bay of California, Mexico, Sea of Cortez.
Besides harboring outstanding flora and fauna, the area is a natural laboratory for studying the ocean.
[2] Krakatoa, Ujung Kulon National Park, Indonesia (Sunda Strait).
[3] Stromboli, Eolian Islands, Tyrrhenian Sea, Italy.

The Galápagos Islands, on the Equator (Pacific Ocean). Situated in extreme isolation at the confluence of three ocean currents, this active volcanic region is unique in the world for the study of evolution. Its original fauna inspired the theories of Charles Darwin.

Along Bay, Gulf of Tonkin, Vietnam. This spectacular seascape is composed of 1,600 steep-sided limestone islands and islets. Virtually uninhabited or disturbed by humanity, the site is also of great interest to biologists.

[1] and [3] The cliffs of the Antrim Plateau and Giant's Causeway, North Channel, Northern Ireland. The basalt landscape is associated with many Irish and Scottish legends.
[2] Naerøyfjord, Norway, Atlantic Ocean. One of the longest and deepest fjords, like its neighbor Geirangerfjord.

Coastal cliffs, Dorset,
England.
The rock formations and
fossils of this shoreline
along the English
Channel provide enor-
mous scope for geologi-
cal study, allowing
scientists to trace the
history of Earth back
some 185 million years,
to the Mesozoic Era.

The Cape Floral region, South Africa (Atlantic Ocean). Almost 20 percent of the flora of the African continent is concentrated here. Exceptionally dense and varied, and wholly endemic to the area, the vegetation is characterized by fynbos, a type of fine brush of great scientific interest.

[1] and [2] The Sian Ka'an Biosphere Reserve, Quintana Roo, Mexico. (Caribbean) Swamps and reefs rub shoulders with tropical forests and mangroves.
[3] Sequoias in Redwood National Park, California, U.S. (Pacific Ocean)—the world's tallest trees cover the coastal ranges.

Shark Bay, W. Australia (Indian Ocean). This natural site is famous, not only for its vast sea-grass beds and dugongs (sea-cows), but also its stromatolites (right-hand page)—layered structures formed by colonies of seaweeds, some of the oldest forms of life.

The Tuareg who dwell in the heart of the Sahara have a saying: *aman, iman* ("Water is life"). Indeed, on every continent, water is the source of drink and nourishment. In all its natural states—flowing, frozen, hot, or bursting from the bowels of the earth in steaming geysers—it shapes the landscape and sustains its populations.

Snows, streams, and floodplains form a wonderful aquatic mosaic, their irrigating effect controlling all life just as organs control a living body. In fact, the humid zones regulate climate and maintain a multitude of biotopes suited to the most varied animal and plant habitats. Did you know that the vast Amazon Basin and its tributaries—Amazonia—possess one-fifth of all the world's freshwater and oxygen reserves? The delta formed by the Ganges and the Brahmaputra, and the banks of the Rivers Congo and Gambia, are no less legendary for their flora and fauna, which include large mammals and carnivores. Myriads of birds flock around lakes or the deltas of the Danube, Guadalquivir, and Senegal.

Lake Baikal (Siberia), amazingly pure and deep, provides evidence of the planet's earliest days. Water is also a powerful sculptor, however; think, for example, of the glaciers of the Andes that unload prodigious icebergs into the southern lakes! The Grand Canyon itself owes its precipitous depth to the erosive effect of the Colorado River, while in other locations runoff water forms petrified falls or seeps down into

Water of Earth, Water of Life

karst (limestone) landscapes to hollow out fantastic caverns. Finest of spectacles, the mighty Zambesi and Iguaçu Falls are wreathed in rainbow-hued plumes of mist while, at Yellowstone, water slides down from the lakes in frozen falls or erupts as boiling geysers.

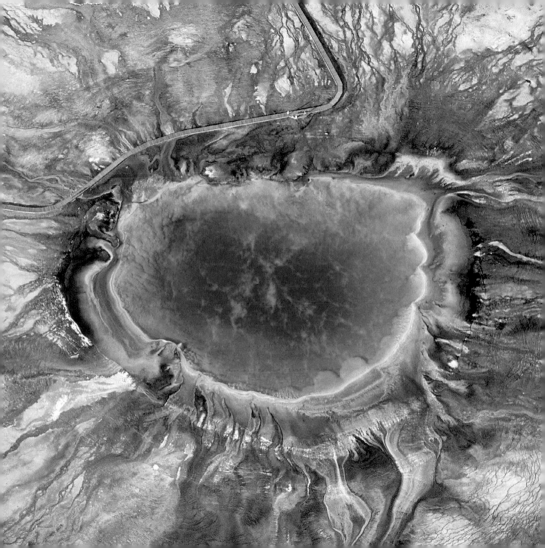

[1] and [2] Wood Buffalo National Park, Northwest Territories, and Alberta, Canada. The world's largest inland delta, with bison wandering freely through the boreal forest.

[3] Nahanni River, Northwest Territories, Canada. This spectacular river carves out incredible karst caves.

The Grand Canyon, Arizona, U.S.
The gorge hollowed out by the Colorado River reaches a depth of nearly 5,000 ft. (1500 m); it allows us to study 2 billion years of geological history. The park also retains traces of prehistoric man.

The Three Parallel Rivers National Park, Yunnan, China. In this mountainous region, the upper course of the Yangtze, the [3] Mekong and the Salouen form precipitous gorges, like those (right-hand page) of Jinsha and [1], [2] Nu Jiang, whose maximum depth is around 10,000 ft. (3000 m).

[1] The Zambesi, Mana Pools National Park, Zimbabwe.
[2], [3], and [4] Central Amazonia, Amazonas State, Brazil.
The Amazon Basin is a treasure-house of aquatic biodiversity. Along the course
of the Rio Negro—[2] a Tucuman palm and [3] the Anavilhanas archipelago.
[4] Fisherman on the Amazon.

The Pantanal, Mato Grosso, Brazil.
An immense, flat wetland watered by the sources of the rivers Cuiabá and Paraguay, the Pantanal forms one of the world's largest and densest freshwater ecosystems, both in terms of flora and fauna.

[1] Iguaçu (Brazil) and [3] Iguazu Falls (Argentina). The semi-circular cataract is 262 ft. (80 m) high and 8,860 ft. (2700 m) wide.
[2] Victoria Falls, Zambia and Zimbabwe. The Zambesi plunges into basalt ravines over 6,000 ft. (2000 m) wide and 300 ft. (100 m) deep.

Lakes and waterfalls at Plitvice, Croatia. In a dolomitic and limestone landscape, water flows elegantly from lake to lake, hollowing out astonishing caves in the karst and sustaining the wolves, bears, and countless bird species native to the forest.

[1], [2], and [3] Lake Malawi, Malawi.
In its clear, deep waters, swarms of endemic fish are major targets in the study of evolution.
[4] and [right-hand page] Lake Turkana, Kenya.
This huge lake, with the highest salt content in Africa, is the breeding ground of Nile crocodiles.

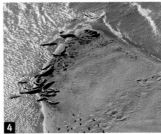

[Following pages] Minerva Terrace, Yellowstone, Wyoming, U.S.
The limestone terraces are wreathed in the steam from boiling water, creating the effect of petrified fountains.

Los Glaciares, Argentina. An area of glacial lakes embedded in the snowbound Andean peaks—three glaciers converge on Lake Argentino, jettisoning enormous icebergs in a continuous roar of sound.

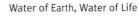

Yellowstone Park, Wyoming, U.S. Old Faithful [1] and Crater Hills [3] are fine examples of the geothermic phenomena responsible for some 300 active geysers in the area. [2] The park also abounds in streams like the Gardiner River.

Ever since its formation, the Earth has gained relief and many mountain peaks... The rocks preserve the memory of this slow development and the spellbinding mountainscapes seem to summon humanity to celebrate the stupendous beauty of nature's works.

Although present-day mountains began to take shape 200 million years ago, fossil-bearing sites hold clues to the amazing evolution of life on earth during even earlier epochs. Fossils of marine animals, for instance, reveal the existence of ancient seas and lagoons, even in the Swiss Alps, while the Rocky Mountains of Canada and the Argentine Desert enable us to follow the development of the earliest vertebrates and the dinosaurs. This was before the Andes and the Himalayas arose 70 million years ago, and before the emergence of all those sheer and snowy summits that inspire us with awe.

The slow erosion of the table mountains of Venezuela and the Brazilian and Ethiopian plateaus has also resulted in spectacular landscapes. Erosion is also responsible for the sandstone crags of Australia and China—and the miraculous karst (limestone) gorges of Central Europe, Asia, Madagascar and North America.

Volcanic activity can brutally transform mountain landscapes, but it is two extinct volcanoes—Kilimanjaro and Mt. Kenya—that have bequeathed Africa its highest peaks. The varied nature of such terrains, their altitude, and their extent enhance the

Mighty Peaks
in Majestic Relief

majesty of the locations; in addition to their geological interest, slopes and undulations display a gradation and extremely rich diversity of plant and animal life, with vegetation consisting primarily of high mountain pasture, temperate or tropical forest, and sometimes vestiges of ancient woodland.

[1] and [3] Talampaya Canyon, La Rioja, Argentina.

[2] Victoria Cave, Naracoorte, mid-South Australia. The fossil-rich sites of Ischigualasto and Talampaya are, like Riverleigh and Naracoorte, prime locations for gathering evidence of the evolution of vertebrates and mammals.

[1] and [2] Dinosaur Park, in the badlands of Alberta, Canada, has yielded the most extraordinary collection of fossils from the Age of Reptiles (75 million years ago). [3] The "prince" of Miguasha Park, Quebec, Canada—a tetrapod fossil from deposits dating to the Age of Fish (370 million years ago).

Landscapes in the Rocky Mountains National Park, Alberta and British Colombia, Canada.
[1] Kootenay National Park.
[2] River Sunwapta, Jasper National Park.
[3] Mt. Assiniboine and Wedgewood Peak, Mt. Assiniboine National Park.
[4] Yoho National Park.

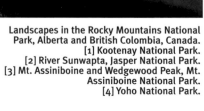

[1] The Jungfrau and the Lauterbrunnen glacial valley, Swiss Alps. [2] The Golden Mountains of Altai and [3] Lake Teletskoye, Siberia, Russia.

[1]–[3] Zanskar Valley, Valley of Flowers National Park, linked with the Nanda Devi Park, India. An enthralling location on the roof of the world. [Right-hand page] In the heart of the Himalayas—Lake Gokyo, in the Khumbu Valley, Everest range, Sagarmatha National Park, Nepal.

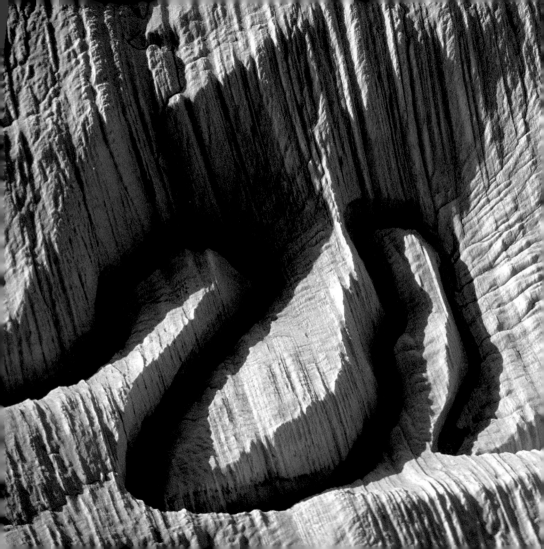

In the northwest corner of the American continent, peaks and glaciers form an awesome landscape that extends across frontiers.
Canada: [1] Tatshenshini-Alsek National Park, British Colombia; [3] Kluane Park, Yukon; U.S.: [2] and [4] Glacier Bay Park, Alaska.

[Preceding pages] Wrangell-St. Elias Park, Alaska, U.S.

Wrangell-St. Elias National Park, Alaska, U.S.

[1]–[3] The first international peace park (Waterton-Glacier) was established in 1932. It combines Glacier Park (Montana, U.S.) with the Waterton Lakes Park in Alberta, Canada.

[Right-hand page] Alpine meadows in Olympic Park, Washington, U.S.

[1] Cathedral Rocks.
[2] Glacier Point.
[3] Northwest face of Half Dome, Yosemite Valley, California, U.S.
This granite range, sculpted by successive glaciations, is the habitat of highly diverse flora and fauna.

The *Tsingy*, or forested limestone spurs, Bemaraha Nature Reserve, Madagascar.
The Manambolo River has carved a spectacular gorge through the rugged karst landscape. These forests being intact, the mangroves and the shores of lakes are the last refuge of rare or endangered birds and lemurs.

[1] Mt. Koryak (volcanic) and [2] Lake Avachinsky, Kamchatka, Russia.
This is an exceptionally volcanic region, where active systems and glaciers interact to shape the landscape.
[3] Tanzania: Mt. Kilimanjaro with savannah elephants.

[1] The Simien Plateau, Ethiopia.
An area shaped by erosion, and a retreat for extremely rare animals like the Simien fox and the gelada baboon.
[2] and [3] The Bungle Bungle range, Purnululu National Park, Western Australia.
The sandstone cones were formed by erosion.

61

Jiuzhaigou Valley, Sichuan, China. Rising to around 15,750 ft. (4800 m), the valley is famous for its magnificent karst landscapes, waterfalls, and variety of forest ecosystems. It hosts a profusion of endangered animals and plants.

[1] and [2] The Wulingyuan region of Hunan, China. Over 3,000 pillars of quartz sandstone create a breathtaking maze among mountain torrents, pools, and gorges.

[3] Giant panda in the Wolong Valley, Sichuan, China. The Sichuan forests are the largest panda sanctuaries.

Boreal forest, tropical forest, temperate forest... Forests occupy nearly one-third of the land mass. Forming veritable living communities populated by plants and animals, their biological diversity is now threatened by mankind—which they have traditionally fed and served.

Nicknamed the "lungs of the planet," forests perform astonishing alchemy with both the earth and the sky, influencing the quality of both soil and atmosphere. The three main types of forest are determined by climate and latitude, but there are others, such as those found on mountainsides.

Boreal forest—or taiga—is the most widespread. Composed essentially of conifers, it forms a belt some 10,000 km (6,250 miles) in length round the sub-Arctic zones in Russia, Scandinavia, and Canada.

On its own, it constitutes one-third of the total world forest. Equatorial forest—humid or dry—is the most rampant. Second in terms of surface, it rules the inter-tropical zone. Humid tropical forest, unfailingly green and luxuriant, is a vast biological treasure-house; vegetation develops at successive layers, the taller trees providing a foothold for lianas, mosses and orchids.

The temperate forests of the Northern Hemisphere are predominantly deciduous. European forest differs from its Chinese or American counterparts by its greater number of species; the latter, however, boast the world's tallest tree—the sequoia.

Forests Like Oceans

Yet natural or "primary" forest, which protects the greater part of biodiversity on the planet, is being progressively hacked down or replaced by "secondary" plantings as part of logging operations. Now it occupies a mere tenth of the surface of the globe.

The ombrophilous tropical forests
of Sumatra, Indonesia.
Scattered between canyons, active volcanoes, and
rice fields, the humid forests teem with flora and
fauna often unique to the location, particularly the
orangutan.

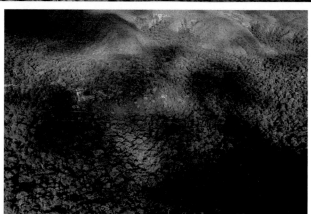

The rainforests of the Noel Kempff Mercado National Park, Bolivia. The park consists of a fantastic mosaic of ever-green rainforest, "gallery" forest, palm forest, dry forest, savannah, cerrado (tropical savannah), and marshland.

[1]–[3] Humid tropical forest, Queensland, Australia.
Mangroves, ferns, and palms flourish in this biotope, together with a wealth of marsupials and songbirds.

[Right-hand page] Camoe River, Ivory Coast.
These islets of dense humid forest are rare at this latitude.

[1]–[3] Natural palm forest in the Mai Valley, Praslin Island, Seychelles.
[3] The area boasts the plant with the world's largest seed—the sea coconut.

70

The savannah of the Serengeti Plains, Tanzania.
Savannah and water-holes attract millions of zebra, gnu, and gazelle
in the annual migration season. This is also the territory of the Masai,
as can be seen from marks scored into the rocks during initiation
ceremonies.

Temperate rainforest, Tasmania, Australia. This type of forest, particularly rich in tree ferns, has now become a rare sight. Lying between mountains and sea, the region was shaped by successive glaciations and has been inhabited by humans since the end of the Ice Age, over 20,000 years ago.

The cool temperate forests of Mt. Shirakami, Honshu, Japan. The last virgin forests of Siebold's beech remain undisturbed by tracks. The mountainsides are populated by black bears, the goat-like serow, and plentiful bird species.

73

The ancient forest of Bialowieza, Poland. This great swath of deciduous woodland and evergreens extends as far as the Belovezhskaya Pushcha Forest in Belarus. It is home to some 300 European bison, plus other rarer fauna including the wolf, lynx, and otter.

The laurel forest on La Gomera in the Canaries (Spain). The humid environment maintains luxuriant vegetation, the last vestige of the forests of the Tertiary Period that covered southern Europe. The same phenomenon is visible in the laurel forest on the Portuguese island of Madeira.

The temperate forest of the Great Smoky Mountains, Tennessee, U.S. Protected from human interference, nearly 800 square miles (200,000 hectares) of forest contain more than 3,500 plant species and almost as many trees as the whole of Europe. It is also the habitat of numerous types of salamander.

Nature rules, when in its wild state and protected from the impact of human civilization. Nonetheless, many isolated peoples live in harmony with their natural environment, which is simultaneously a threat and the provider of necessities. This environment is at the root of powerful cultural traditions.

Races are known as "autochthonous" if they have been attached to their territory since time immemorial—they number today around 300 million individuals. Although modern civilization is always knocking at their door, they frequently manage to preserve their traditional way of life and are bonded with nature by a cosmogony that is both sacred and material. For instance, the Maoris regard the volcanic Mt. Tongariro (New Zealand) as a living landscape that connects them with their Polynesian ancestors.

Large areas of our world heritage depend on local societies to guard the ecosystem and maintain its balance, be they Indian tribes of Central America and Amazonia or reindeer-breeding Lapps from within the Arctic Circle.

Sometimes custom (based on oral tradition) rules the reservations, as on Rennell Island in the Solomons. In Australia, a scattering of Aborigines perpetuate their activities and exercise their rights in a way that best preserves their natural and ethnological patrimony. As Jean Malaurie observes, "humanity's second wind will come from these peoples... who have preserved their sense of heritage and give a meaning to their relationship with nature."

The World of Traditional Peoples

On the other hand, the presence of the Miccosukee tribe may well interfere with the restoration of the "River of Grass"—the Everglades of Florida. Safeguarding an imperiled heritage can pose delicate dilemmas when combined with the need to preserve a living ancestral culture.

Kakadu Park, Northern Territory,
Australia.
Plateaus of sculpted rock and floodplains
form a landscape inhabited for 40,000
years. Here, from Neolithic hunters and
fishers to the Aborigines, mankind has
left an unequalled archeological legacy
illustrated by rock paintings.

The Uluru monolith, Uluru-Kata Tjuta Park, Northern Territory, Australia. Dominating the sandy plain, it is part of the belief system of the Aborigine people, one of the world's oldest societies. The Anangu maintain their traditional rights and customs in the park.

The active volcano Ngauruhoe and the Mahuia Rapids, Tongariro National Park, New Zealand. For the Maori people, mountains symbolize the link between earth, sky, and man. For this reason, Tongariro was the first cultural landscape on the World Heritage List.

The Bandiagara plateau, Dogon territory, Mali.
The jutting sandstone cliffs carry the imprint of the Dogon people's living social traditions. Tradition governs architecture in particular—homes and storehouses, *toguna* (meeting places for the men), altars, and sanctuaries.

85

The Air and Agadez mountains, Sahara, Niger.
This former volcanic massif isolated in the Ténéré Desert has been inhabited since Neolithic times, as witnessed by the petroglyph of the giraffe. The area forms part of the territory traversed since time immemorial by the nomadic Tuareg.

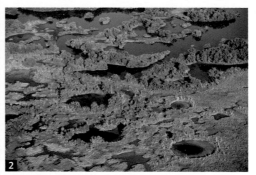

[1] and [2] Florida, U.S.: the swamps and mangroves of the Everglades, and [4] alligator prints.
Home to the Miccosukee tribe, the Everglades form part of an extraordinarily varied, but fragile, aquatic ecosystem and are a refuge for manatees and a multitude of birds and reptiles.

[3] and [5] Natural landscapes of Laponia, Sweden. The Arctic Polar Circle, with its mountains, moraines, and ice-rivers, is of great geological interest. The Saami people carry on their ancestral way of life, particularly the summer migration of reindeer herds, a tradition dating back to prehistoric times.

Wonderful
Buried Treasures

Like Tom Thumb back in the mists of time, human beings and their ancestors have left traces of their passage all over the earth. Fossils, skeletons, constructions, and primitive art forms are all footprints of unknown worlds, the ghosts of which return to haunt the collective imagination.

Prehistory begins with the appearance of the first hominids. Their traces can be found in the paleontological deposits of eastern and southern Africa, which chronicle over 4 million years of evolution. For Africa is the cradle of humanity. The Awash Valley (Ethiopia), for instance, has yielded prolific remains, among them those of a small female Australopithecus who has captured the popular fancy—"Lucy," who died at the age of 20 some 3.18 million years ago. More recently, the genus *Homo* has come to light, notably in Tanzania (*Homo habilis*, c. 2 million years); he reached Europe through Spain (1 million years) and appeared in Asia as *Homo erectus* before becoming our own *Homo sapiens* ("wise man") after 100,000–150,000 years colonizing the planet. Since then, the story of Man has come down to us through artifacts and the rock art through which he strove to depict his experiences. Carvings and paintings are found everywhere—from Asia to America, from the Far North to the Kalahari via the Sahara, which was then a savannah still roamed by innumerable animals.

If *Homo habilis* was capable of manufacturing knapped stone tools, it is above all the traces of the Neolithic Period (7,000–3,500 BC) that enable us to learn more about the

The Earliest Traces of Man

tribal lifestyles of our ancestors. Vestiges of their habitations and activities survive on every continent, as well as tumuli (funeral mounds) or impressive megaliths...The techniques used to build the latter were in fact perpetuated into the sixteenth century on Easter Island and in Senegambia.

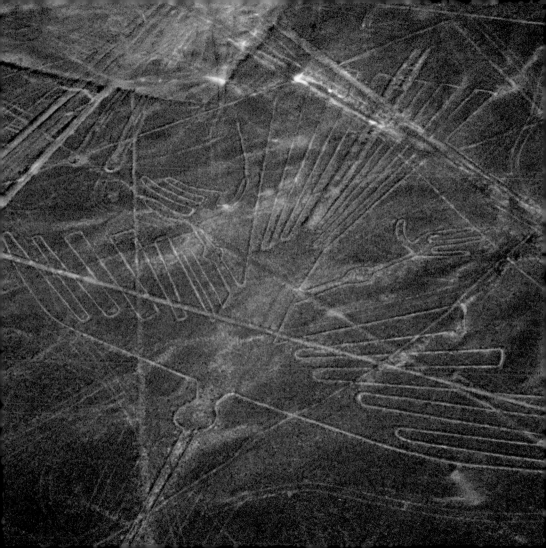

Megalithic structures: [1] Avebury and [2] Stonehenge, Wiltshire, England. Evidence of cult ceremonies from prehistoric times, these prehistoric monolithic circles form two sanctuaries whose astronomical significance remains uncertain.

[1] Tomb and [2] carved megalith at Newgrange.
[3] Neolithic tomb at Knowth, Boyne Valley, Ireland. The prehistoric sites of the Boyne Valley make up Europe's largest megalithic complex. The monuments are of a varied nature—funerary, sacred, or profane.

Megalithic structures in the San Augustín Archeological Park, Colombia.
Gods and mythical animals bear witness to the culture of the northern Andes from the 1st through the 8th century. This is the largest collection of megalithic monuments in South America.

[1] and [3] Tarxien, and [2] Mnajdra temples, Malta.
These Bronze Age megalithic temples (c. 3,000–2,000 BC) are all the more remarkable given the severely limited resources of their builders.

The moai of Rapa Nui or Easter Island, Chile.
These huge human statues were erected between the
10th and 16th centuries. They are remnants of an original
culture that was developed, with no extraneous influence, by a Polynesian population that settled on the
island in the 3rd century.

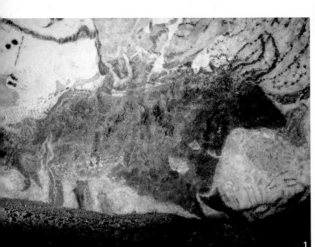

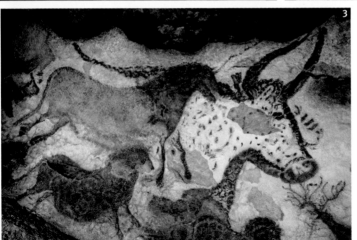

[1]–[3] Cave paintings of bison, Lascaux II, Vézère Valley, France. In total, the site contains 25 painted caves and 147 archeological deposits.
[Right-hand page]
"Stenciled" wall paintings from the Cueva de las Manos (Cave of the Hands), Rio Pinturas, Patagonia, Argentina.

Rock art sites of Tadrart Acacus, Sahara, Libya. In this sandstone massif littered with stone circles—funerary monuments—rocks and caves teem with carvings and paintings dating from between 12,000 BC and the 1st century AD. They form a major record of changes in climate and lifestyles.

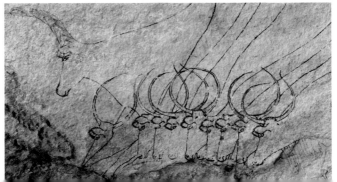

Rock paintings at Tassili n'Ajjer, Sahara, Algeria. Like Tadrat Acacus, its extension, this prehistoric rock art site set in an extraordinary landscape features thousands of drawings and carvings executed with unparalleled skill. They date from 6,000 BC through the early centuries AD.

103

Petroglyphs from Alta Fjord, Norway.
This profusion of paintings and carvings by
peoples dwelling on the edge of the Arctic
Circle between 4,200 and 500 BC provides
detailed information about life in the Far
North during prehistoric times.

Petroglyphs at Tanum in North Bohuslän, Sweden.
The enormous range of subjects—boats, people, and miscellaneous artifacts—gives us a clear picture of life and beliefs in North Europe during the Bronze Age (2,500–1,000 BC).

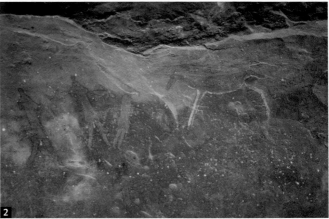

[1]–[3] Rock paintings from the uKhahlamba Mountains, Drakensberg, South Africa. For 4,000 years, caves and rock shelters served as a canvas for artists. [Right-hand page] Rock art from the Sierra de San Francisco, Lower California, Mexico Dating from between 100 BC and 1300 AD, this represents the culture of a vanished people.

Agriculture was born around the sources of major rivers in the Middle East before spreading to fertile basins like those of the Tigris, the Euphrates, and the Nile. Gradually, highly structured societies replaced agricultural communities, inventing writing and an urban lifestyle. Civilization had arrived!

The story begins in early antiquity, in the East, around 3,500 BC. On the grain-producing plains, men constructed artificial hills known as "tells," which bear witness to continuous building activity from the seventh or eighth millennium BC; they remained in use as trading centers for a long time, as civilization overflowed into Mesopotamia and Egypt, then into Elam (Iran), the Indus Valley (Pakistan), Crete, and Asia Minor. Its progress can be gauged by the diffusion of cuneiform writing and hieroglyphs and most especially by the increasing scale of building projects. Constructing a city was tantamount to establishing an empire, as in the case of Assyria, Babylon, pharaonic Egypt, and the Hittite empire in Turkey. From the port of Byblos (Lebanon), the Phoenicians opened up maritime trading routes across the Mediterranean and subsequently founded Carthage. Later, land-based trade with Arabia, Egypt, and Syria-Phoenicia assured the prosperity of the fabulous Nabatean cities of Petra and the Negev Desert.

New centers of civilization continued to arise in the thousand years after Christ, with the establishment of the Etruscans on the Italian peninsula, the Persian empire of Cyrus the Great, and the state formed by Thracian horsemen on the banks of the Danube... And

Magnificent Civilizations of the Orient

archeology continues to yield precious clues about events in the East, such as the expansion, in the early Christian era, of the Parthian empire and the Kingdom of Axum, or the golden age of the Sassanids, the Omayyads, and the Hammadid Berbers.

[1] The stepped pyramid of King Djoser and [2] interior of the Mastaba of Ti, Saqqarah Necropolis, Memphis, site of the pyramids of Gizeh, Dahshur, Egypt; 3rd millennium BC.
[3] Isis and Horus—detail from the Temple of Isis, Phile, Nubia, Egypt.

[1] and [2] Temple of Isis at Phile, 4th to 2nd century BC.
[3] Entrance to the temple of Luxor, Thebes, and Necropolis, Egypt; 14th to 13th century BC.

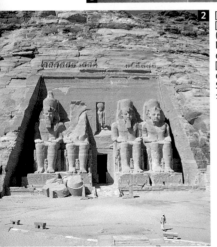

[1] Statue of Ramses II.
[3] Temple of Luxor (Thebes) and necropolis, Egypt; 14th to 13th century BC.
[2] The Great Temple of Ramses II at Abu Simbel, Nubia, Egypt; 13th century BC.

[1] Avenue of the Sphinx, Luxor (Thebes) and necropolis, Egypt; 14th to 13th century BC.
[2] Colossal statues from the great temple of Ramses II, Abu Simbel, Nubia, Egypt; 13th century BC.

113

[1]–[3] and [Left-hand page]
Persepolis, capital of the Acheminid
Empire, Iran; 6th to 5th century BC.
[1] Bull—capital from the Chamber
of the Hundred Columns.
[2] Procession of nobles and digni-
taries, east staircase of the Apadana
(audience hall).
[3] Staircase of the Apadana.
[Left-hand page] Darius I, founder
of Persepolis in 518 BC.

[Following pages] The royal necropolis of Meroe (270 BC–350 AD),
Mt. Gebel Barkal, Sudan.

[1] The Crusader fortress at Byblos, Lebanon.
The Phenician city, at the height of its power from the third millennium before Christ, played an indispensable role in the development of trade and civilization in the Mediterranean, notably by exporting its alphabet.
[2] and [3] Remains of the Phoenico-Punic city of Kerkouan, Tunisia; 6th to 3rd centuries BC.

Canyon and remains of the Nabatean city of Avdat, on the incense route, Negev Desert, Israel; 3rd century BC to the 2nd century AD. Avdat is one of the four great fortresses of the Negev, guarding the trade route between the Arabian Peninsula and the Mediterranean.

Rock tombs and obelisks of the Nabatean city of Petra, Jordan.
The sculpted buildings of Petra—a vital center of the caravan trade—
were constructed in the labyrinth of mountains between the Red and the
Dead Seas. The golden age of the city was between the 1st century BC
and the 1st century AD.

The ruins of Anjar, Lebanon.
Founded in the early 8th century by Caliph Walid I, the ancient city displays signs of the rigorous and refined planning developed by the Omayyads.

The oasis and ruins of Bahla Fortress, Oman. The brick fort was constructed on a stone base. Its impressive dimensions underline the power of the Banu Nabhan, who ruled the area from the 12th century until the end of the 15th century.

I n Greek mythology, the Phoenician princess Europa was abducted by Zeus and carried off to Crete; her brothers, after a fruitless search, are said to have founded several cities there. This was how the Ancients thought civilization was brought from East to West... across our universal mother, the Mediterranean.

In addition to an incalculable archeological heritage, Ancient Greece has also bequeathed us philosophy, the arts and sciences, and democracy. From Rome we have inherited the idea of the republic, law, yet more art and architecture, city planning, and toward the last days of the Empire Christianity, elevated to the status of official religion after years of persecution.

The earliest center of Hellenic civilization was Mycene, which flourished between 1600 and 1200 BC; according to the *Iliad* of Homer,

it was the Mycenean king, Agamemnon, who led the Greek expedition against Troy.

The famous Greek cities began to blossom from around 800 BC. They created their alphabet, established the Olympic Games and the Sanctuary of Apollo at Delphi, and founded independent colonies all around the Mediterranean. Athens, in particular, reached her apex during the classical era (500–350 BC). Later, Alexander the Great took up the torch, transmitting Hellenistic culture throughout his vast empire, from Macedonia to Egypt and the Indus River.

Rome—which became a republic in 510 BC—was already staking her claim, however. She assimilated the heritage of Greece, making the latter a Roman province in 146 BC. The Empire was established in 27 BC. By the early second century AD, Rome controlled Europe from Britain to the Black Sea, and

The Greeks and the Romans—Pillars of the West

Asia as far as the Euphrates and North Africa, with over 3,000 miles (5,000 km) of fortified frontier to hold back the barbarians. The last western Roman emperor abdicated in 476, leaving Constantinople as the capital of the eastern Empire.

[1] and [2] The Lion Gate, Mycenae, Peloponnesus, Greece.
The city was at the heart of Mycenaean civilization between the 15th and 12th centuries BC, profoundly influencing classical Greek culture.

[3]–[6] Paphos, Cyprus. According to mythology, the birthplace of Aphrodite, to whom a temple was dedicated some 1200 years before Christ. Paphos was enhanced with countless monuments from the Hellenistic period to the Byzantine age.
[3] Byzantine fort reconstructed by the Turks.
[4] Tombs of the Kings (4th century BC).
[6] Basilica of Agia Kyriaki or Chrysopolitissa.

Delos, Cyclades Islands, Greece. Delos was sacred to Apollo—who is said to have been born here—but also a powerful port. Successive civilizations left their imprint on the island from the 3rd millennium BC to the Paleochristian era. A fine example is the Terrace of the Lions (7th century BC).

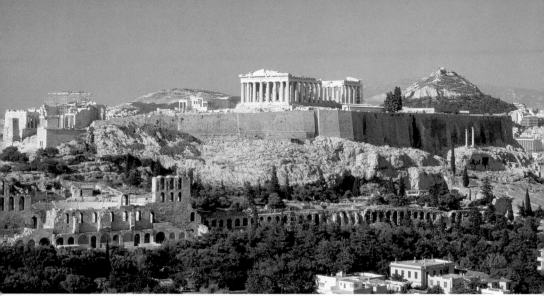

The Parthenon and the Acropolis, Athens, Greece.
The supreme masterpieces of the Acropolis were executed on the orders of Pericles in the 5th century BC. The Parthenon, a marble temple dedicated to Pallas Athene, became the symbol of the transmission of classical Greek art and culture, a process still very much alive today.

[1] The Parthenon, the Acropolis, Athens, Greece.
[Left-hand page] and [2] The tholos of the sanctuary of Athene Pronaia; and [3] the Temple of Apollo, Delphi, Mt. Parnassus, Greece. Famed for its oracle, the shrine of Apollo attracted pilgrims from all over the Greek world, whose unity it symbolized in the 6th century BC.

[1] The theater at Epidaurus, Peloponnesus, Greece. Dating to the 4th century BC, it is one of the glories of Greek architecture.

[2] and [3] The Sanctuary of Zeus (the Altis) at Olympia, Peloponnesus, Greece. Remains can be seen of structures used for competitions in the Olympic Games, inaugurated in 776 BC and repeated every fourth year.
[4] Entrance to the Olympic stadium.

Remains of the Roman thermal baths at Hierapolis (Pamukkale), Turkey.
The city was established besides springs rich in calcite by the rulers of Pergamon in the late 2nd century BC. Besides the Roman baths, the ruins include fine Greek monuments and temples.

The Tomb of Antiochus I, on the summit of Nemrut Dag, eastern Turkey. Littered with the broken heads of colossal divinities, the conical tumulus was erected for the king of Commagene in the 1st century BC.

[1] and [3] The Villa Adriana, Tivoli, Italy.
One of the gems of classical architecture and inspired by Egypt, Greece, and Rome, this "ideal city" was conceived in the 2nd century AD by the Roman Emperor Hadrian.
[2] Butrint, Albania.
A former Greek colony that subsequently became a Roman, then Byzantine, city.

136

Forum Romanum and Trajan's Column, Rome, Italy.
Dating from the 6th century BC, the Forum was the commercial, political, and religious center of Rome, first under the Etruscan kings and later the Republic and the Empire. The column was not erected until 113 AD; It stands in the forum of Trajan, further to the north.

[1]–[3] and [Right-hand page] Pompeii, Italy.
The Roman colony, a flourishing commercial center, was buried during the eruption of Vesuvius in 79 AD.
[2] The amphitheater (80 BC) could seat 80,000 spectators.
[3] The House of the Fawn, decorated with frescoes and mosaics (2nd or 3rd century BC).
[Right-hand page] Mercury Street.

[1] Remains of Roman gold mines at Las Médulas, Spain (1st century AD).

[2] The Roman aqueduct at Segovia, Spain (1st century AD).

[3] Amphitheater, Roman city of Arles, France (1st century AD).

Pont du Gard, France.
This marvel of technology formed
a section of the Nîmes Aqueduct
built by Roman engineers around
19 BC. It is 164 ft. (50 m) high, over
900 ft. (275 m) long, spans the
River Gardon on three levels.

Palmyra, Syrian Desert. A caravan oasis sited at the crossroads of major civilizations, Palmyra was once a flourishing city and an important center of culture. Greco-Roman remains from the first and second centuries show the influence of both Persia and local tradition.

[1]–[3] Baalbek, Lebanon.
A Phoenician city renamed Heliopolis in the Hellenistic Era, Baalbek became a Roman colony in the first century BC, when imperial Roman architecture was at its height.
[1] Temple of Bacchus.
[2] Temple of Jupiter Heliopolitanus.
[3] Temple of Mercury.

[1] and [2] Masada, Judean Desert, Israel.
A powerful symbol of the ancient kingdom of Judea, the fortified palace was constructed by Herod the Great in the 1st century BC in classic Roman imperial style. It was the site, in 73 AD, of the last stand by Jewish patriots against the Roman legions.
[Right-hand page] The Chalcidicum and theater, Leptis Magna, Libya (2nd to 3rd century AD).

[1] to [3] Leptis Magna, Libya.
A former Phoenician trading post that passed into Carthaginian and later Roman hands, Leptis was considerably embellished by the emperor Septimus Severus, who was born there. During the 2nd and 3rd centuries, it was one of the finest cities of the Roman Empire.
[1] Medusa head.
[2] Forum of Septimus Severus.
[3] Basilica of Septimus Severus.

[1] Cyrene, Libya. A former Greek colony and capital of Cyrenaica, Cyrene fell under Roman influence in the 1st century BC.
[2] Sabratha, Libya. Established by the Phoenicians to trade with the African interior, the city was Romanized and rebuilt in the 2nd and 3rd centuries AD.

The amphitheater of El Jem, Tunisia.
Testament to the glory of the Roman Empire, this arena is the largest in North Africa, built in the 3rd century AD to accommodate 35,000 spectators.

[1] and [2] Remains of the Punic city and [3] the Antonine Baths, Carthage, Tunisia. Carthage was already a commercial power by the 6th century BC. The Romans destroyed it in 146 BC, but refounded and absorbed it into the Roman Empire as capital of the new province of Africa.

[1], [2], and [Right-hand page] Volubilis, Morocco.
This ancient Berber city was founded in the 3rd century BC. As capital of Mauretania, it became an important outpost of the Roman Empire. Enjoying numerous monuments and superb mosaics, its finest hours were in the 2nd and 3rd centuries after Christ. [Right-hand page] Basilica.

Throughout the world, civilizations have blossomed and known their hour of glory, only to sink back into darkness. Their spiritual legacies, however, run like a thread through the culture of later nations, underpinning their foundations, while their tangible bequests to posterity are their physical remains— modest or magnificent—whose significance archeologists strive to interpret.

unearth cultures as diverse as those of ancient Chinese cities, the Brahman and Buddhist societies of Sri Lanka, the Sukothai style of Siam, Hindu and Indo-Muslim architecture, and traces of Karakorum, the capital of Genghis Khan. Excavations have also resurrected the splendor of the African empires of Mapungubwe and Great Zimbabwe, and the once prosperous Tanzanian seaports that traded with Arabia, Persia, and China.

In the North, we have traced the Vikings of Scandinavia to Canada and rescued from oblivion relics of Icelandic culture such as the sites at Kernave (Lithuania), which represent 10,000 years of human habitation.

Again, the wealth of pre-Columbian cultures emerges as we exhume the totems of Canadian Indians, American pueblos, and the

Since the first excavations at Pompeii in 1748, one buried city after another has

Lost Cities and Empires

been restored to the light of day. These patiently rediscovered ruins, hundreds or thousands of years old, serve to enrich the whole of mankind; their legacy is boundless and transcends frontiers. In Asia, the remains of former capitals are revealing vanished kingdoms as archeologists

clusters of extraordinary monuments left by the great builders of the cities and ceremonial centers of Chavín and Teotihuacán, the Maya civilization, the empire of the Incas, and other once dominant peoples. Each of these sites provides us with unique evidence about the culture that created it.

The pre-Columbian site of Chavín, Peru.
This ancient ceremonial center perched up in the Andes gave its name to the Chavín civilization that developed between 1500 and 300 BC. Its architecture is distinguished by stone constructions decorated with bas-reliefs and heads in the round.

[1]–[3] The sacred city of Teotihuacán, Mexico. Teotihuacán, meaning "place where gods are created," was laid out between the first and seventh centuries using a rigorous system of geometry and symbolism. [2] and [3] The Pyramid of the Sun, dedicated to [1] Tlaloc, the rain god.

[1]–[3] Tiwanaku, Bolivia.
The spiritual and political center of the Tiwanaku culture was at its height from the 6th through 10th centuries. This unique civilization ruled a powerful empire in the southern Andes.
[1] Temple of Kalasasaya.
[2] Sculpted monolith.
[3] Gate of the Sun.

[1]–[3] The hypogea at Tierradentro, Colombia. These underground tombs are evidence of the culture evolved by a civilization from the northern Andes between the 6th and 10th centuries. Of vast dimensions, they are decorated with motifs similar to those found in dwellings of the period. [2] Funerary sculpture of a serpent.

Cliff Palace, Mesa Verde, U.S.
This edifice marks the supreme development of the Anasazi people, who built numerous rock villages between the 6th and 12th centuries. Cliff Palace consists of over 100 rooms and several circular kivas used for rituals.

Chaco village and ceremonial center, New Mexico, U.S. Chaco Canyon was a major cult center of the Ansazi people between 850 and 1250. Its public buildings and the ceremonial kivas tell us much about group culture among the Chaco.

[1] and [2] Tikal, a Mayan city and cultural center in Guatemala, inhabited from the 6th through 10th century BC.
[1] The acropolis.
[2] Temple of the Great Jaguar.
[3] and [Right-hand page] The Maya city of Copán, Honduras. Boasting an acropolis and five monumental squares, it flourished between 300 and 900 AD.

[1]–[3] The Mayan city of Uxmal, Mexico.
The ceremonial site of Uxmal marks the culmination of Mayan art and architecture (early 8th to late 10th century AD). The city had a population of up to 25,000. [1] Devin pyramid. [2] Double-headed jaguar guarding the governor's palace. [3] Palomar or dovecote.

Xochicalco, Mexico. The art and architecture of this fortified political, religious, and commercial center (650–900 AD) reflects the cultural fusion that took place after the collapse of the great Mesoamerican states of Teotihuacán, Monte Albán, Palenque, and Tikal.

[Following pages] The sacred Mayan-Toltec city of Chichen-Itzá, Mexico. A chac-mool (stylized reclining figure) and the pyramid of Kukulkán (Quetzalcoatl), known as El Castillo; 10th to 13th century AD.

163

[1]–[3] The Mayan sanctuary of Palenque, Mexico. Still largely buried in forest, Palenque peaked between the 6th and 8th century. [1] The Palace. [2] Human head in stone. [3] Temple of the Cross.

[1] and [2] The city of El Tajín, Mexico. At the height of its power in the early 13th century, El Tajín ("Place of Thunder" in the Totonac language) enjoyed immense influence in Central America. [1] Pyramid of Los Nichos, a masterpiece of astronomical and symbolic architecture. [2] Jaguar bas-relief.

167

Relics of the Haida people on SGaang Gwaii, Queen Charlotte archipelago (Haida Gwaii), British Colombia, Canada. Decimated by disease in the 1880s, the abandoned village of Ninstints is littered with old constructions and funerary or commemorative totems from the past, though the Haida culture still lives on today.

The sacred stronghold of Machu Picchu, Peru. Construction of this Inca city—whose name means "Ancient Mountain" in the Quechua language—began in the mid-15th century. It is spectacularly integrated into the landscape of the Andean Cordillera at an altitude of just under 8,000 ft (2,430 m) amid the tropical forest of the Upper Amazon Basin. According to the poet Pablo Neruda, "Here we have one of the greatest wonders of South America... yet another miracle." (*The Heights of Machu Picchu*).

The ancient city of Sigiriya, Sri Lanka. The Lion Rock, dominating the jungle, incorporates the citadel of King Kassyapa (477–495), who made Sigiriya his capital. Access is via a series of stairways and galleries, emerging between the paws of a colossal lion constructed of brick and sculpted plaster.

Orkhon Valley, Mongolia.
This land of nomadic shepherds with their famous yurts (tents) once belonged to Karakorum, capital of the Mongol empire in the 13th and 14th centuries. Among the ruins—bounded by stone tortoises—are stupas commemorating Buddhist sages, dating from 1586 onward.

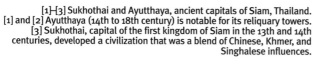

[1]–[3] Sukhothai and Ayutthaya, ancient capitals of Siam, Thailand.
[1] and [2] Ayutthaya (14th to 18th century) is notable for its reliquary towers.
[3] Sukhothai, capital of the first kingdom of Siam in the 13th and 14th
centuries, developed a civilization that was a blend of Chinese, Khmer, and
Singhalese influences.

Polonnaruwa, a former capital of Sri Lanka. This Buddhist center retains Brahmanic monuments erected by the Chola sovereigns who made it their capital from the 11th century. Polonnaruwa also contains monumental ruins of the garden city of King Parakramabahu (12th century).

175

Wonders
of Sacred Art

Confronted by the grandeur of nature and in a search for transcendence, humanity has designated certain locations as possessing spiritual significance. Thus the planet is littered with sacred sites and holy places designed to bring together the finite and the infinite, the divine and the human.

Regions with striking landscapes or harsh, difficult terrain—islands, mountain peaks, caves, or canyons—are favorite sites for initiating mankind into the mysteries of the universe and the divine. Most cultures, despite their huge diversity, have their holy mountains where a link exists between earth and heaven, with the abode of their ancestors, or with the center of the earth: Mt Sinai, for instance, was the site of the divine revelation to Moses, while the Imperial cult in China centered on Mt. Taishan.

Forests are equally numinous—the mysterious habitation of gods, or of ancestors who were lost there, they have become objects of veneration and identity symbols. Water is inseparable from life. Symbolic of purity, it is at the heart of religions and purification rites. As a result, there are innumerable sacred springs, wells, oases, rivers (like the Ganges), and lakes, frequently associated with the passage from life to death.

Many sites are charged with the memory of prophets, saints, or sages who founded religions—Buddhism, for example—or, even more, recollections of a divine manifestation; this explains why Jerusalem is a holy city for the three great monotheistic religions.

Such locations assume the role of sanctuaries: incorporated into buildings and sometimes even the starting point for the construction of a city, they develop into places of pilgrimage. Pilgrim trails in turn become enshrined in folk memory, as with the route leading to the shrine of St. James in Santiago de Compostela.

Sacred Sites

The Giant Buddha of Leshan, Mt. Emei, Sichuan, China. The first Chinese Buddhist temple was built in the 1st century on Mt. Emei—a place held sacred in the Buddhist religion, which had already permeated the Far East. The 233-ft. (71 m) statue was hewn out of the hillside during the 8th century.

Mt. Taishan, Shandong, China.
This holy mountain was the object of
an Imperial cult for almost two
millennia. Evidence of the nature
worship practiced in ancient China, it
has inspired numerous artistic and
literary works throughout the history
of the country.

[Following pages] The Giant Buddha
of Leshan, Mt. Emei, Sichuan, China—
the world's largest statue of the
prophet

The Longmen Caves, Henan, China. Thronging with stone sculptures, its caves and niches entirely devoted to Buddhism, Longmen is evidence of the flourishing artistic culture of the Northern Wei and the Tang dynasties (316–907) which has exercised a profound influence on Chinese art.

[1] Dagoba Ruvanvelisaya, the Holy City of Anuradhapura, Sri Lanka.
The city has grown up around a scion of Buddha's "Tree of Awakening," brought here in the 3rd century BC.
[2] and [3] Sacred city of Kandy, Sri Lanka.
A major pilgrimage site, it includes the temple of the Buddha's Tooth.

Shinto shrines and Buddhist temples at Nikko, Japan. The mausoleum of the Tokugawa shoguns, particularly the Toshogu shrine (c. 1636), blends harmoniously with the landscape. It reflects on one of the principles of Shintoism, the traditional Japanese religion that includes a cult of nature.

Sacred sites and pilgrim tracks in the mountains of Kii, Japan. Enfolded by dense forests with their network of fast-flowing streams and waterfalls, Mt. Kii, meaning "Land of Purity," is at the center of a religious movement that integrates traditional Shintoism with Buddhism, which was introduced to Japan in the 6th century.

[1], [2], and [Right-hand page] Jerusalem, the Holy City of Judaism, Christianity, and Islam.
[1] The Holy Sepulcher, built on the site of the crucifixion and resurrection of Christ.
[2] The Dome of the Rock, a sacred place of Islam, recognized by all three religions as being the site of the intended sacrifice of Isaac by Abraham.
[Right-hand page] The Wailing, or Western, Wall, sole relic of the Jewish temple.

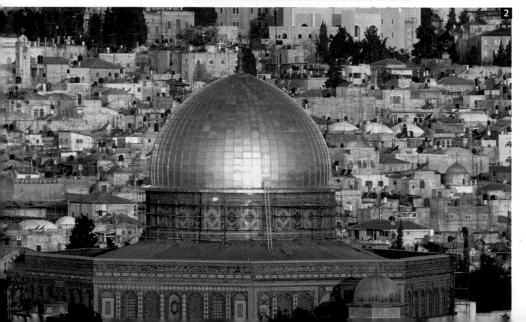

[1]–[4] The Vatican City, Holy See of the Roman Catholic Church. The world's largest religious building stands within the smallest sovereign state. Saint Peter's Basilica occupies one of the Seven Hills of Rome and marks the spot where the apostle was martyred; along with Saint Paul, Saint Peter is considered the founder of the Catholic Church. The basilica houses inestimable art treasures and unites the genius of Bramante, Raphael, Michelangelo, Bernini, and Maderno.

[1] and [4] Saint Peter's Basilica, with dome (1546–64 and 1590).
[2] The Vatican Library.
[3] Piazza of Saint Peter (1656–67).

Mont Saint Michel, France.
A pilgrimage site since the Middle Ages, the Gothic-style Benedictine abbey (11th to 16th centuries) is known as the "Wonder of the West." It stands on a small, rocky island perilously exposed to ferocious tides—but is under the protection of Saint Michael, Prince of Angels.

Saint Catherine's Monastery, Mt. Sinai, Egypt.

This is one of the oldest Christian monasteries (6th century), huddled at the foot of Mt. Sinai: the holy mountain known as *Horeb* to Jews and *djebel Musa* to Muslims. According to the Old Testament, Moses received the tablets of the Ten Commandments, here.

The monolithic churches of Lalibela, Ethiopia. The monastic city of Lalibela, a 13th -century "New Jerusalem," is the Holy City of the Christians of Ethiopia. Eleven churches have been hewn out of the rock, including the spectacular church of St. George, whose roofline is level with the earth.

South portal of the Gothic
cathedral of Notre-Dame de
Chartres, France, 12th to 13th
centuries

Churches and cathedrals are part of the familiar landscape of Christianity. Witness to the spiritual influence of this faith, these monuments with their soaring towers and crosses have become, over some twenty centuries, a massive repository of the world's art treasures.

Christianity was only allowed to construct its first great religious buildings after the conversion of the Emperor Constantine in the early fourth century. Two basic plans for ecclesiastical edifices emerged at that time—the rotunda and, more particularly, the basilica, which in its elongated form became the norm almost everywhere. Soon afterward, Constantinople gave birth to Byzantine art, essential to the development of form and style in the Middle Ages.

In the field of religion, architecture was dominated by the demands of liturgy. In Europe, the choir was placed at the east end from the fifth century; later, the Carolingian Renaissance led notably to the cult of saints and the introduction of the crypt.

Romanesque architecture (950–1100s) can be distinguished by its use of stone vaulting inspired by Ancient Rome and by the addition of transepts and chapels. Gothic art developed in turn in the Île-de-France during the twelfth century, emphasizing luminosity and height thanks to its use of ogival cross-vaulting. The art form of the cathedral was now established, combining architecture, stained glass, and sculpture in a vast liturgy of stone.

In contrast to the centralized plan of the Renaissance, the Counter-Reformation

The Genius of Christianity

preferred a cruciform plan surmounted by a dome, designed to express the glory of God as also depicted in Classical and Baroque art.

Christianity has always incorporated the skills of its converts. In their turn, missionaries abroad entrusted European designs to local craftsmen, who reinterpreted them in a blend of traditional and naive styles.

The Piazza del Duomo, Pisa, Italy; 11th to 14th centuries.
The four buildings around which the lives of the faithful revolved were also four architectural masterpieces — the cathedral, the campanile (bell tower), known as the Leaning Tower, the baptistery, and the Camposanto (cemetery). All had considerable influence on the history of Italian art.

[1]–[3] Paleochristian monuments, Ravenna, Italy; 5th to 6th century AD.
A former capital of the Western Roman Empire (fifth century AD) and subsequently of Byzantine Italy, Ravenna rejoices in architectural and art treasures where Greco-Roman influences coalesce and East merges with West.
[1] Oratory of St. Andrea.
[2] Church of St. Vitale.
[3] Mausoleum of Galla Placidia.

[1] Aachen cathedral, Germany, incorporating the Palatine chapel (late 8th century) added under the patronage of Charlemagne.
[2] Romanesque Ottonian church of St. Michael, Hildesheim, Germany, 1010–20.
[3] Gothic cathedral, Cologne, Germany; 1248–1880.

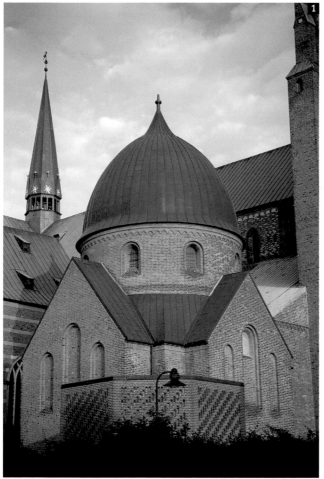

[1] Gothic cathedral of Roskilde, Denmark; 12th, 13th, and 19th centuries.
Scandinavia's first brick-built cathedral, whose style was imitated throughout Northern Europe.

[2] Gothic cathedral of Our Lady of Burgos, Spain; 13th, 15th, and 16th centuries.

Medieval church of Boyana, Bulgaria; 10th, 13th, 19th centuries.
Composed of three distinct buildings, the 13th-century portion is decorated with frescoes that form a major collection of East European medieval paintings.

[1] Churches of Jvari and [2] Samtavro, Mtskheta, Caucasus, Georgia.
Fine 11th-century examples of the arts and culture of the former kingdom of Georgia.
[3] The cathedral of St. Sophia, Kiev, Russia (11th century) was designed to rival the building of the same name in Constantinople.

[1] Durham Cathedral, England; late 11th–early 12th century. A gem of Norman architecture, built by Benedictine monks.

[2] and [right-hand page] Gothic cathedral of Notre-Dame de Chartres, France; the 12th to 13th century. The archetype of French Gothic, and an object lesson in the use of ogival vaulting, sculpture, and stained glass.

[1] The papal palace, Avignon, France; fortress that became the seat of the papacy for much of the 14th century. [2] Palace of Tau, the former archiepiscopal palace of Reims, substantially reconstructed in the 1600s. [3] Gothic cathedral of Notre-Dame de Reims, France; 13th century.

206

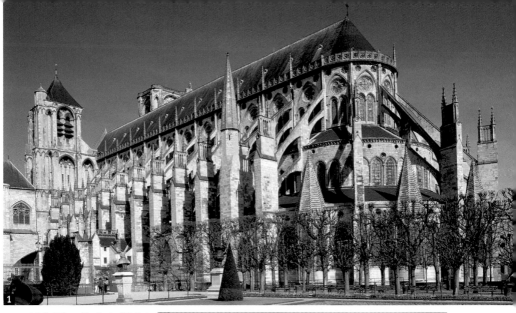

[1] Gothic cathedral of Saint-Étienne de Bourges, France; late 12th to 13th century.
[2] Gothic cathedral of Notre-Dame d'Amiens, France; 13th century. Its interior dimensions make it the largest medieval building in France.

[1] Byzantine wall-painting from the monastery of Ayios Ioannis (St. John) Lampadhistis, Kalopanayiotis, Troodos mountains, Cyprus; 11th century.
[2] Painted church, Moldavia, Romania.
Byzantine fresco from the 15th to 16th century.

Cathedral of St. James, Sibenik, Croatia; 1431–1535. Built entirely of stone, it is evidence of cultural exchanges between Dalmatia, North Italy, and Tuscany, while the sculpted frieze of 71 portraits marks the transition from Gothic ecclesiastical architecture to that of the Renaissance.

[1]–[6] The missionary churches, convents, and monasteries of Goa, India were responsible for the dissemination of Manueline art, Mannerism, and Portuguese Baroque in all the surrounding countries of Asia.

[1] Basilica of Bom Jesus (1605); the burial place of St. Francis Xavier.
[2] 17th-century church of St. Francis of Assisi.

[3] Convent of St. Monica (1628).
Goa's earliest religious foundation for women
[4] Church of the Immaculate Conception; 1614.
[5] Church of Our Lady of the Rosary .
St. Francis Xavier, who landed at Goa in 1542, regularly preached here.
[6] Church of St. Gaetan; c. 1640.

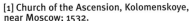

[1] Church of the Ascension, Kolomenskoye, near Moscow; 1532.
Erected on Imperial domain to mark the birth of Ivan IV (the Terrible), this was one of the first Russian Orthodox churches to incorporate pavilion roofs with brick and stone supports.

[2], [3], and **[Right-hand page]** Pilgrimage church of Wies, Bavaria, Germany; 1745–1754.
A masterpiece of Bavarian rococo with ornate stucco decoration, this was the brainchild of architect Dominikus Zimmermann, constructed to receive pilgrims attracted by a miraculous wooden statue of the Scourged Christ.

[1] and [2] Stave church (*stavkirke*) at Urnes, Sogn og Fjordane, Norway; 12th to 13th century.
The wooden church is one of Scandinavia's architectural gems, its style borrowed from Celtic, Roman, and Viking sources.
[3] Timber church at Haczow, Malopolska, Poland; 14th to 19th centuries.

The *pogost,* or sacred enclosure, on Kizhi Island, Lake Onega, Karelia, Russia. The churches are from the 18th century the octagonal tower, from 1862. The Church of the Transfiguration with its cascading domes is built around a core of three stepped octahedrons is one of the finest examples of traditional Russian wooden architecture.

Wooden churches of the Chiloé archipelago, Chile; 17th through 19th century.
These churches are distinctive for their blend of European and native designs and techniques. Exceptional examples of Latin American churches of the type, they are the result of a tradition that was begun in the 17th and 18th centuries by itinerant Jesuit missionaries and which has been continued ever since.
[1] Church, Castro.
[2] and [right-hand page] Church, Acao.
[3] Church, Chonchi.

The monk, by definition, lives apart, secluded from the world and under strict discipline. Nevertheless, the monastic movement flourished throughout the Christian world. Monasteries became spiritual, intellectual, and artistic centers that contributed to the foundations of European civilization.

From the very beginnings of Christianity, religious fervor inspired swarms of hermits and cenobites (monks living in communities) to settle in the area east of the Mediterranean where, in the fourth century, St. Pacomo set up the first model monastery in the Egyptian desert. In the Near East this model gave rise to original art forms and traditions in Coptic Egypt, Syria, Armenia, and the Caucasus, while Byzantine influence extended to Greece, the Balkans, and even Russia. The first Western monastery was founded in Gaul by St. Martin as early as 361.

It was, in fact, the monks who would convert Europe, with the monastic Rule of St. Benedict, developed in the Carolingian era, introducing order and cohesion. This unity emerged in the layout that grouped the complex around the cloister; it evolved at Saint-Gall and was adopted by both the Benedictines of Cluny and the Cistercians to become the enduring norm. These orders were the great builders of the Middle Ages: they developed and disseminated Romanesque and Gothic architecture, adapting it to local traditions as they went along. The Franciscans and Dominicans were equally important as cultural missionaries from the 1200s; they ushered in the

Masterpieces of Monastic Art

epoch of the first great Italian painters and, later on, the art of the Renaissance.

A new injection of enthusiasm was given to European monasticism by the Counter-Reformation, which adopted Italian classicism in the design of its stately abbey-palaces.

Ruins and cemetery of the Skellig Michael Monastery, Ireland; c.7th century.
The choice of site—a small, craggy island well away from the coast—is evidence of the dedication and asceticism practiced by the earliest Irish Christians.

Irish monks went on to convert parts of Europe.

The basilica of St. Francis of Assisi, Italy; 13th century.
The basilica crowning the tomb of St. Francis is a tour de force of medieval art. Several of the early Italian masters contributed to its decoration, including Giotto, who was responsible for the frescoes of the upper basilica.

[1] Church of St. Clement.
[2] Monastery of St. John the Theologian, Ohrid, Macedonia; 13th century.
Ohrid, converted by SS. Cyril and Methodus, passed on Slavic culture in the Balkans and encouraged the use of the Cyrillic alphabet. The monastery houses one of the most significant collections of Byzantine icons.

[3] Ghelati monastery, Kutaisi, Georgia; 12th through 17th centuries. A fine example of the former kingdom's triumphal era.

[4] and [5] Rila monastery, Bulgaria; 10th to 18th, 19th centuries. Marking the tomb of the hermit St. John of Rila, this monastery was a major Slavic cultural center for Bulgaria in the Middle Ages.

[1] and [2] Monastery of Nea Moni, Island of Chios, Aegean Sea, Greece; 11th-12th century. [3] Daphni monastery, Attica, Greece; 11th-12th century. These scattered monasteries are characterized by their mosaic-laden cupolas, typical of the second Golden Age of Byzantium.

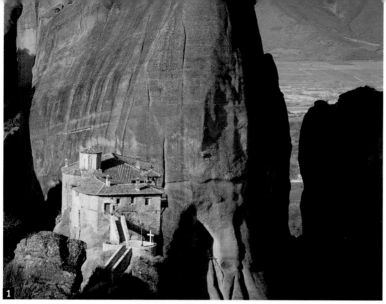

The monasteries at Meteora, Greece. As early as the 11th century, anchorite monks established themselves here on these virtually inaccessible "heavenly pillars." The monasteries contain outstanding post-Byzantine frescoes of the 16th century.
[1] Roussanou monastery; 16th century.
[2] Varlaam monastery; 1536–44.

Basilica of St. Mary Magdalene on the Mount at Vézelay, France; 12th century. Since medieval times, the heights of Vézelay have attracted pilgrims to the relics of St. Mary Magdalene. The church of this Benedictine monastery is renowned for both its glorious architecture and sculptures in the Burgundian Romanesque style and links with the Crusades.

[1] The Royal Monastery of Santa Maria d'Alcobaça, Portugal; 12th century.
Gothic art at its best.
[2] The Romanesque abbey church of Saint-Savin-sur-Gartempe, France, which incorporates the crypts of Saint Savin and Saint Cyprian. A Benedictine foundation with memorable wall-paintings.

[1] Fortified monastery of Malbork, formerly belonging to the Teutonic Order; 13th century. Archetypal brick castle.
[2] and [3] Flemish Beguine convent, Bruges, Belgium; 13th century. The Beguines were an independent order of nuns.

[Left-hand page] Dominican Convent of Santa Maria delle Grazie, Milan, Italy; 15th century. The convent was redesigned by Bramante and decorated by Leonardo da Vinci, whose Last Supper adorns the refectory.

[1] Convent of St. Francis of Assisi, Italy; 13th century.

[2] Royal Monastery of Santa María de Guadalupe, Spain; 14th to 15th century. Dedicated to the Virgin Mary, the influence of this Mudejar gem extended even to the New World.

Cistercian abbey, Fontenay, France; early 12th century. Founded by Saint Bernard on an isolated and marshy site, the Burgundian abbey is a model of Cistercian architecture—austere and destined for a perfectly self-contained, communal regime.
[1] and [3] Cloisters.
[2] Refectory.
[4] Dorter and Infirmary.
[5] Chapter House.

[1] and [2] Hieronymite monastery, Lisbon, Portugal; 1502–19. The pinnacle of Manueline art. [3] The fortified monastery of Novodievitchi, Russia; 16th to 17th century. A stunning example of Muscovite baroque linked to the history of Russia and the Tsars.

Lavra of the Holy Trinity and St. Sergius, Sergiev Posad, Russia; 15th to 18th centuries. The Lavra—Orthodox monastery—was founded by hermit Sergius of Radonezh, the patron saint of Russia. Overlooking the fortress is the cathedral of the Assumption, with paintings by Andrei Roublev and containing the tomb of Boris Godunov.

The Splendors of Islam

Dating back fourteen centuries, the civilization of Islam extends from the Atlantic to the Pacific, from Morocco to Indonesia, and from Spain to Africa. It is renowned for the wealth and diversity of its arts and architecture, which embody a close bond between the spiritual and the temporal or urbane.

Islamic conquerors, setting out from Arabia after the death of the prophet Mohammed (632), rapidly forged a sprawling empire that was soon parceled up into caliphates, some of which acquired enormous power. This explains why many major cities are associated with Islamic centers; the ruler would have been anxious to impose the religion of the victors to control both the city and the souls of its people.

The first great mosques amounted simply to a huge courtyard lined by porticos and blanked off in the direction of Mecca by a wall. Known as the "Arab" plan, it is ubiquitous in the Maghreb, Spain, and Iraq. From the Omayyad era (661) detailed decorative techniques and the addition of ancillary buildings—mausoleum, school, etc.—became yardsticks of the power of the ruler and prosperity of the community.

It was, however, through contact with pre-Islamic civilizations that the architecture developed. Thus stone triumphed from Spain to Iraq, but baked brick is more usual from Iraq to India. The minaret made its appearance in Abassid Iraq (eighth century), to be followed by the cupola and the porch, both propagated by the eleventh–century Seljuks; these features became typical of Iranian and Turko-Persian mosques. Finally, Moghul architecture in India adopted the distinctive bulbous cupola, while the Ottoman Empire perfected a style influenced by Byzantium. Nevertheless, on the fringes of the Islamic world—Indonesia, Malaysia, China, Africa — religious buildings tended to follow traditional designs, incorporating little Islamic influence.

The Great Mosque of Kairouan, Turkey; ninth century, redesigned several times.
A key base for the Arab conquest and conversion of North Africa to Islam, the garrison town of Kairouan was founded in 670. The Aghlabid emirs made it their capital in the ninth century. They reconstructed the Great Mosque which, with its 17 naves, supported a forest...

... of marble and porphyry columns; it became the model for numerous others in the Maghreb. Even today, Kairouan remains the leading holy city of that region.

239

The medina (market) of Fez, Morocco. Founded in the 9th century, Fez is home to the world's oldest university.
[1] The Bab Boujeloud gate; 12th century.
[2] The Sahrij medersa (school); 14th century.
[3] Kutluk Timur minaret, Kunya-Urgench, Turkmenistan; early 11th century. Emblem of the Islamic culture of Khorezm Province.

The minaret and ruins of Djam, Afghanistan; late 12th century. At a height of 213 ft. (65 m), the minaret, with its double spiral staircase, is an example of Ghorid architecture. The complex decorative element consists of Kufic inscriptions in baked brick, partially highlighted by blue tiles.

Islamic Cairo, Egypt.
Cairo is one of the oldest and most prestigious cities of Islam. Founded in the tenth century, it was the capital of the Fatimid and later the Ayyubid caliphs, reaching its peak under the Mameluks in the 1300s.

Throughout this period and beyond, Cairo
rejoiced in all that was finest in Islamic art.
[1] and [5] El-Azhar mosque; 972.
[2] and [4] Ibn Touloun mosque; 879.
[3] Mosque and medersa of Sultan Hassan;
1356.

The Great Mosque of Divrigi, Anatolia, Turkey; 1228–1229.
The mosque and its hospital were constructed on the initiative of the emir Ahmet Shah shortly after the Turkish conquest. The mosque is noted for the technique of the cupolas and the exuberance of its decoration and portals.

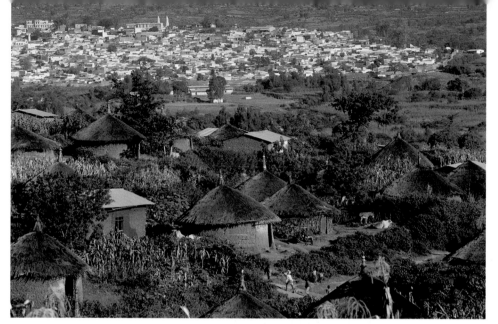

The fortified city of Harar Jugol, Ethiopia.
Capital of the Harari kingdom in the 16th century, Harar developed into an Islamic city steeped in African traditions. It is considered the fourth most holy city of Islam, boasting 102 shrines and 82 mosques, including 3 from the 10th century.

[1] and [2] The Qutub Minar, Delhi, India; early 13th century.
This tall minaret in red, elaborately-fluted sandstone watches over some remarkable remnants of Indo-Islamic architecture, including adaptations of Brahman temples.
[3] and [Right-hand page] Mausoleum of Oljeitu, Soltaniyeh, Iran; 1302–1312. The double cupola surmounting a hexagonal structure marks a revolution in Persian and Islamic architecture.

[1]–[4] Mosques at Timbuktu, Mali. The medersa and the three large mosques date from the city's era of prominence—the 15th and 16th centuries—when it was a major center for the propagation of Islam in Africa and one of the intellectual capitals of the continent.
[1], [3], and [4] Djingareyber mosque; early 14th century.
[2] Koranic University of Sankoré; 15th century.

[5] Tomb of Askia, Gao, Mali; 1495.
Askia Mohammed, Emperor of Songhai, established Islam as the official Imperial religion and constructed this striking pyramidal tomb in his capital, in addition to several mosques.

Duuring the first few centuries AD, India and China were the civilizing forces of Asia. The philosophies of both included a cosmology founded on the concept of universal harmony. This view of the universe found expression in art through the symbolism that dominates the design of temples.

The Hindu religion, derived from Brahmanism, has been an indistinguishable part of Indian history for thousands of years. Its highly codified, sacred architecture envisages the temple as a model of the cosmos—at the center resides the divinity, represented by the symbol of Shiva; the upper stories are the various heavenly levels; and the tower represents the axis of the universe. This principle was unfailingly followed, even in rock temples, and attained its ultimate perfection in the tower shrine. These towers reached unparalleled size in the countries of south and south-east Asia that converted to Hinduism, such as the mountain temples of Angkor, or to Buddhism—Borobudur, for instance.

Buddhism, in fact, founded 25 centuries ago in India, adopted the basic tenets of the Hindu architectural model. There were certain differences, however; Buddhism revels in figurative decoration and its use of the stupa—funerary monument, cosmic symbol, and aid to meditation.

The spread and influence of Buddhism was to prove immense. The Chinese honed its art forms and employed them to ennoble its traditional timber architecture. The pagoda, for example, borrowed from both the Indian stupa and the multistoried pavilion of the Han era. Temples of the great Chinese religions—Taoism, Confucianism,

The Myriad Temples of Asia

and Buddhism—benefited from similar treatment. As a conquering power, China passed on its religion and its building techniques; in Korea, the pagoda became a stone monument, whereas Japan opted for more radical designs, remarkable for their wonderful array of roofs.

[1] Buddhist rock temple, Ajanta, India; 2nd–1st century BC–5th–6th century AD.
[2] The Golden Temple of Dambulla, Sri Lanka. This cave-temple has been a major pilgrimage site for 22 centuries.
[3] Lumbini, birthplace of the Buddha (623 BC), Nepal.

Ruins of the Buddhist monastery of Takht-i-Bahi, Swat Valley, Pakistan; 1st to 7th centuries.
With its stupa courtyard and monumental niches enshrining exquisitely draped statues, this monastery set in the high valleys of the Indus is one of the most impressive remnants of the Gandhara civilization.

The great Buddhas and the Bamyan Valley, Afghanistan; 1st through 13th centuries.
This valley of Central Asia crossed by the Silk Route and dotted with fortified villages stood at the meeting-place of the Indian, Hellenistic, Roman, and Sassanid cultures that inspired the Buddhist art of Gandhara. The two large standing Buddhas (3rd-5th century), blown up by the Taliban in 2001, led pilgrims to the surrounding rock shrines. The valley was converted to Islam in the 10th century.

Palace of Potala, Lhasa Valley, Tibet, China; 17th century.
The Winter Palace of the Dalai Lama was founded in the 7th century on the 12,139-ft. (3,700 m) Red Hill. Reconstructed to the "round city" design favored by Tibetan Buddhism, it has become a religious and historic landmark.

The Buddhist shrines at Kyongju, Korea; 7th to 9th century.
A unique variety of Buddhist art developed in the kingdom of Silla. At Kyongju, where necropolises rub shoulders with pagodas and temples, it finds expression in architecture and sculpture.

The Buddhist temple of Borobudur, Java, Indonesia; 8th to 9th century. A fusion of mountain temple and mandala, its levels correspond to those of the hill, the summit forming its natural center.

The temple is on three levels. The base consists of five concentric square terraces; next are three circular platforms with 72 pierced stupas containing images of the Buddha. The whole is crowned by a monumental stupa. The design is a quintessential example of Buddhist art taking its inspiration from India.

[1] Temple of the Sun, Konarak, India; 13th century.
A Brahman temple representing the chariot of the sun god, Surya.
[2] Kailasha rock temple, Ellora Caves, India; 8th century.
No less than 34 shrines—Buddhist, Brahman, and Jain—have been hollowed out of the basalt cliff.

[1] Rock temples sacred to Shiva, Mahabalipuram, India; 7th century, Pallava Dynasty.
[2] Dravidian temple of Brihadisvara, Thanjavur, India; 11th century; Chola Empire.
[3] Hindu temple of Virupaksha, Pattadakal, India; c. 740, Chalukya Dynasty.

Angkor, Cambodia; 9th to 15th century.
Angkor Wat and Angkor Thom were two capitals of the Khmer Empire. These temple-cities teem with masterpieces of Khmer architecture inspired by Hindu buildings in India.
Angkor Thom; 13th century

[1] South entrance.
[2] Bayon Temple; 13th century Hindu (formerly Buddhist Mahayana) temple.
[3] The Phimeanakas Hindu temple; 10th to 11th century.
[4] Temple of Angkor Vat; 12th century.
Hindu temple of Vishnu, later adapted for Buddhism.
[5] Elephant Terrace.

Buddhist and Hindu monuments in Katmandu Valley, Nepal.
Among the foothills of the Himalayas, the crossroads of Asia's great civilizations, the royal cities, palaces (*durbars*), and religious buildings of the Katmandu Valley reveal...

... Nepalese art and architecture at its very finest.
[1] and [3] Buddhist stupas at Swayambhu.
[2] and [6] Temple of Krishna Mandir, Durbar Square, Patan; 1668–1734.
[4] Sculpture from the Hindu temple of Changu Narayan; 1702.
[5] Nyatapola temple, Durbar Square, Bhaktapur; 12th to 18th century.

Humanity has doubtless always made a ritual of death. Ceremonies accompany the passage of the departed toward the unknown regions beyond, while the cult of the dead preserves their memory around their ashes. From this arises an art form—funerary art —the earliest kind practiced by humanity.

From the simple prehistoric circle of stones to the noblest mausoleum, a place of burial is a landmark for posterity. There, by manipulating space, memory strives to halt the flight of time. Thus tumuli, heaped above tombs, stood out in the landscape as the earliest form of homage to the deceased; later on, stone—a material synonymous with resistance to decay—was associated with the complex cosmology of megaliths, menhirs, and dolmens. Finally came colossal pyramids and other monumental tombs.

From early times, the quest for eternal life dictated the mysterious laws of sacred architecture governing Amerindian or Egyptian funerary chambers or the mausoleums of Chinese emperors. It encouraged the search for beauty and harmony, the use of symmetrical forms, with the sumptuous decoration surrounding the dynasts entombed among their fabulous treasures.

Ancient rock tombs or the royal wood-and-reed sepulchers of Buganda, Indian garden-tombs, sensational necropolises, or simple cemeteries are all abodes of eternity stamped with the mark of the civilizations that created them.

Other monuments have been constructed to celebrate great turning-points in history, or

Extraordinary Tombs

have been preserved for their role as witnesses. At the sites of unspeakable catastrophes such as Auschwitz or Hiroshima, ruins form a sacred perimeter designed not only to condemn the ravages caused by man's cruelty and destructive power, but also to maintain his hopes of a lasting peace.

[Right-hand page]
Mausoleum of the first Qin emperor, Xi'an, China. Qin, who died in 210 BC, lies surrounded by an army of terracotta soldiers.
[1] Jingling mausoleum, Ming Dynasty, Beijing, China; 1463.
[2] The Oriental Qing tombs, Zunhua, China.

Jelling cemetery, Denmark. Here, the burial ground has not altered since the conversion of the Danes to Christianity in the 10th century. Tumuli and runic stones—pagan and Christian—crowd around the church and its cemetery.

Memorials of the life of Martin Luther in Wittenberg, Germany. [1] Church of St. Mary, where Luther preached the Reformation from 1543. This movement provoked a schism in Christianity and gave birth to Protestantism. [2] Residence of Luther.

Tomb of Hamayun, Delhi, India; 1570. Hamayun was the second Moghul emperor; his mausoleum was constructed by his widow, Biga Begum.

A superb instance of early Moghul architecture, the tomb of Hamayun established the model of the garden-tomb that culminated in the Taj Mahal. The site became the necropolis of the Moghul Dynasty, and contains some 150 tombs.

[1] and [2] The Hiroshima Peace Memorial: Genbaku Dome, Japan.
The Dome was the sole building to remain standing after the dropping of the first atomic bomb on August 6, 1945. It figures on the World Heritage list as "a stark and powerful symbol of the most destructive force ever created by mankind, but also expressing the hope for world peace and the ultimate elimination of all nuclear weapons."
[3]–[5] Taj Mahal, Agra, India; 1631–1648.

The Taj Mahal, a vast white mausoleum incrusted with semi-precious stones, pays homage by the Moghul emperor Shah Jahan to his favorite wife, Mumtaz Mahal, and is the iconic example of Islamic art in India.

Wonderful Cities

Steeped in memories and history, capital cities proclaim the identity of nations in the world arena. Dozens of these magnificent landmark locations, whether centuries old or mere decades young, contribute their architectural treasures to the common heritage of humanity.

A capital city is both the symbolic center of a nation and the focal point of its power and activity, from which the state draws its underlying legitimacy. Inextricably linked with historical events of the highest importance, the capital is a strategic point in all great developments—political, religious, and artistic. Its cultural heritage, wealth of monuments, design, and architectural diversity bear witness to its pre-eminence among cities, while the eclecticism acquired by its urban landscape resembles a patina imposed by the passage of,

perhaps, thousands of years. As seats of princes or commercial powers rejoicing in the trappings of success, capitals span the most glittering eras of human civilization with consummate ease.

Some of these capitals have had to make heroic stands against threats to their primacy—Lima or Quito, ravaged by earthquakes and, even more so, Warsaw, reconstructed in identical fashion after the Second World War to perpetuate its historical continuity in the collective memory.

New states demand new capitals. This is the chance for the most inspired planners to implement political and cultural ideas on an innovative scale. Instances are the multicultural capitals of the New World and the wonders of the twentieth century, including

Sublime Capitals

the "white city" of Tel Aviv, a remarkable 1930s architectural complex, and, more recently, Brasilia, founded on an empty site at the heart of the country as a fresh affirmation of its unity—and in the shape of a bird.

282

[1] and [2] Vilnius, capital of Lithuania. Historic center.
[3] Tallinn, capital of Estonia. Old town.
[4] and [5] Riga, capital of Latvia. Historic center.

Warsaw, capital of
Poland.
Market square and
historic center,
reconstructed on
identical lines after
the Second World
War.

[1] and [2] Moscow, capital of Russia.
[1] Basilica of St. Basil, Red Square; 1818.
[2] The Kremlin; 14th to 17th century.

285

[1]–[5] Prague, capital of the Czech Republic. Quarter known as the Old Town.
[1] Bell tower of Our Lady Victorious; towers of Our Lady Before Tyn.
[3] St. Nicholas Church.

[2] and [4]
Charles Bridge
on the river
Vltava. and the
castle quarter,
with St. Vitus
Cathedral.
[5] Quarter
known as Little
Town.

[1]–[3] Vienna, capital of Austria.
[1] Graben.
[2] Burgtheater.
[3] Hofburg Palace.

Budapest, capital of
Hungary.
Banks of the Danube
and the Buda castle
quarter.

289

Brussels, capital of Belgium. [1] Grand-Place
Berne, capital of Switzerland. [2] Old town
Edinburgh, capital of Scotland. [3] The castle

London, capital of
England.
The Tower of London,
beside the River Thames.

[Following pages] Paris,
capital of France.
Banks of the Seine.
Pont-Neuf with eques-
trian statue of Henry IV at
the western end of the Île
de la Cité.

[1]–[5] Paris, capital of France.
[1] The roofs of the Conciergerie (Île de la Cité), the Pont-Neuf, and the Louvre. (Right Bank)
[2] The Conciergerie, Île de la Cité; late 13th to 14th century.

[3] Eiffel Tower (Left Bank); 1889.
[4] Left Bank.
[5] Île de la Cité and Notre-Dame.
In the background is the dome of the Panthéon (Left Bank).

[1] Sanaa, capital of Yemen. Old town.
[2] Damascus, capital of Syria. Grand Mosque of the Omayyads in the old town; 8th century.
[3] Valetta, capital of Malta.

[1]–[2] Tunis, capital of Tunisia. Medina [1] Mosque of Youssef Dey and [2] Grand (Ez-Zitouna) mosque.

[1]–[3] Santo Domingo, capital of the Dominican Republic. This colonial city was founded in 1498, six years after the discovery of Hispaniola by Christopher Columbus. [1] Cathedral of Santa Maria La Menor; 1524–1544. [2] Alcázar de Colon; 1509. [3] Statue of Christopher Columbus on the Plaza Colon; 1886.

[1]–[3] Havana, capital of
Cuba Old town.
[1] Parque Central.
[2] Gran Teatro and dome
of the Capitol.
[3] The Prado.

[1] and [2]
Mexico City,
capital of
Mexico.
Historic center.
[1] Palacio de
Bellas Artes;
1904–1930.
[2] Metropolitan
Cathedral; 16th
to 19th century.
The largest
cathedral on
the American
continent.

[1] Xochimilco, Floating Gardens. The canals and artificial islands on what was once Lake Texcoco testify to the technological skills of the Aztecs.
[2] Panama City, capital of Panama Panama Viejo (Old Panama) was the first European colony on the Pacific coast of the Americas (1519), but was abandoned in the mid-17th century.

[1] and [2] Lima, capital of Peru; historic center.
[1] Church and monastery of San Francisco; 17th
–early 18th century.
[2] Plaza de Armas.

[3] and [Right-hand page] Quito,
capital of Ecuador; historic center.
The decoration of the church of the San Francisco monastery
marks the beginning of the 18th -century "Quito baroque"—a
blend of Spanish, Italian, Moorish, Flemish, and native styles.

I n Paris, Victor Hugo wrote: "Certain cities are Bibles in stone." Brimming with history and art, they are showcases for a vast cultural heritage. Two hundred and fifteen of them, these wonders of five continents are thus affiliated to the Organization of World Heritage Cities (OWHC).

Many cities, in fact, include a site on the World Heritage List. Capitals of vanished empires or fallen kingdoms, strongholds of commerce or financial giants, religious or cultural centers, they boast a rich and colorful past. The opulence of their public and private buildings today bears witness to past economic triumphs and the soaring artistic and architectural impulses that were their driving force down the ages.

A city is an indivisible whole. For this reason, the preservation movement targets not only the most remarkable monuments, but also entire quarters—historic centers, "old cities," and even "museum cities," whose designs and urban fabric encapsulating vistas of fine buildings afford exceptionally complete and well-preserved illustrations of centuries-long development. Such a city's identity can be "read" in its brick and stone, its structures and architectural solutions, and its successive choice of styles.

At the heart of cultural exchanges, these eternal cities have made their presence felt far and wide, extending their influence over whole regions and even across national frontiers. Their fame in human memory remains linked to the blossoming of a

Eternal Cities

national culture—Nara in Japan, or Guimarães in Portugal, for instance—or to the emergence of philosophical or literary movements such as Bamberg and the Age of Enlightenment, as well as to the reputation of artists who flourished there, like Salzburg, birthplace of Mozart.

[1]–[3] Nara, Imperial capital of Japan in the 8th century. Its Buddhist temples and Shinto shrines demonstrate how the development of Japanese art and architecture was influenced by China and Korea. [1] Horyu-ji temple. [2] and [3] Stone lanterns and Todai-ji Buddhist temple; 745.

[1] and [2] Kyoto, Imperial capital of Japan from the 8th century through 1868.
The timber-based religious architecture and garden designs developed here exercised considerable influence throughout Japan and the world.
[1] Kinkaku-ji ("Golden Pavilion") Zen temple; 14th century.
[2] Kiyomizu-dera temple; 780 BC–1630 AD.

[1] and [2] Hue, Imperial capital of Vietnam from 1802 through 1945.
[1] Gate of the Citadel.
[2] River of Perfumes.

[1]–[3] Ping Yao, Shanxi
Province, China
Archetypal Han city;
14th-20th century.
[1] Roofs of the
Buddhist temple.
[2] Market.
[3] City walls.

Ispahan, Iran.
Mosque of Sheikh Lotfollah,
Meidan Emam square; early
17th century.

310

[1] and [3] Fatehpur Sikri, India.
Ruins of the former capital
(1571–1585) of the Moghul Empire.
[2] Thatta, Pakistan.
The old capital received constant
facelifts from the 14th-18th centuries.
Here, the mausoleum of Jani Beg and
Ghazi Beg Tarkhan.

[1]–[3] Novgorod, first capital of Russia in the 9th century. Major Orthodox religious center and focal point for the development of Russian architecture.
[1] Church of St. George; mid-14th century.
[2] Church of St. Peter and St. Paul; 1406.
[3] Cathedral of St. Sophia; 1045.

Bruges, Belgium. The medieval city was one of Europe's foremost commercial and cultural centers and the cradle of the Flemish Primitive School.

[1] Telc, Czech Republic; historic center with Renaissance houses.
[2] Lübeck, Germany. Fortified brick gateway of the Holstentor (1478), emblem of Lübeck, the former capital of the Hanse and once the commercial metropolis of northern Europe.
[Right-hand page] Weimar, Germany. Kavalierhaus of the Schloss Belvedere (1826). The cultural influence of Weimar was immense, attracting Bach, Goethe and Schiller.

[1] Salzburg, Austria. Its baroque opulence and fortress underline the splendor of this ancient city-state, which was also the birthplace of Mozart.
[2] Graz, Austria. Fief of the Habsburgs, the city has benefited since medieval times from local and regional influences in art, architecture, and culture.

[1] and [2] Lyon, France.
Capital of the Three Gauls founded by the
Romans in the 1st century BC, Lyon has been
a model of urban development for centuries.
[1] Notre-Dame-de-Fourvière; 1872–1896.
[2] Place des Terreaux.
[3] Strasbourg, France; Grande Île and
Vauban Dam on the River Ill.

[1]–[3] Siena, Italy.
The city is built around the historic
center, the Piazza del Campo.
[1] Torre del Mangia (1325–1344) and
Palazzo Publico (1293–c. 1310).
[2] Basilica di Santa Maria dell'Assunta;
c. 1215–1263.
[3] Piazza del Campo and Fonte Gaia
(Gaia Fountain).

[4] San Gimignano, Italy. Ostentatious symbols of power and wealth, the tower houses of the historic center were built in the Middle Ages by the noble families who ruled the city.

[1], [2], and [Right-hand page] Florence, Italy. Artistic center par excellence for six centuries, Florence has come to symbolize the Renaissance. It was the city of the Medici and the setting for the work of Giotto, Brunelleschi, Botticelli, Michelangelo...
[1] Palazzo Pitti and Fontana del Carciofo; late 16th–early 17th century.
[2] Basilica di Santa Maria del Fiore and cupola; 1296–1492.
[Right-hand page] Basilica di Santa Croce; 1294 and 19th century.

[Left-hand page] Mistra, Greece. Renowned as the "Wonder of Morea" during the Renaissance, the city developed around the fortress of the Frankish warlord William II of Villehardouin. It was abandoned in 1832.

[1] and [2] Split, Croatia. Split stands on the Dalmatian coast and was built on the ruins of the Palace of Diocletian (295–305), which survive among the later buildings of the historic center.

[1], [2], and [Right-hand page] Istanbul, capital of Turkey. The Bosphorus peninsula was the seat of the capital of the Eastern Roman Empire. (Constantinople), the Byzantine Empire (Byzantium), and finally the Ottoman Empire (Istanbul). [1] and [Right-hand page] Blue Mosque or Sultan Ahmet Camii; 17th century. [2] Hagia Sophia; 6th century.

From its Latin derivation, "civilized" means being the member of a "civis" (town or city). Nevertheless, the urban dweller stubbornly dreams of the ideal environment. Europe took steps to achieve this aim—the city of complete harmony. By adopting designs in which beauty was paramount, the great builders of the continent infused their cities with a spirit that has served as a model throughout the world.

The modern city, meticulously planned from every aspect, was born at the hands of the humanist theoreticians of the Renaissance, who inaugurated the architectural principle of allying the aesthetic and the practical. Applied in Italy from the fifteenth and sixteenth centuries, this led to the invention of monumental perspective and regularized designs. From Pienza or Vicenza to Florence or Rome, the art of city building was entrusted to the finest architects whose reputation extended not only across Europe but also the Atlantic. Italian models were perpetuated in the succeeding centuries through the baroque or classical styles, wherever cities were redesigned (for example, Nancy and Bath); rebuilt (the Noto Valley, Lisbon); or created from scratch (St. Petersburg).

Spain turned the "ideal city"—the *Civitas Dei* ("city of God")—into a reality, by establishing the world's first purpose-built University City and exporting to Latin America the models developed on the Iberian Peninsula.

With the arrival of mass manufacturing, however, scientific and technological progress encouraged utopian reformers and philanthropists to conceive a type of "universal" community that would be the basis of brand-new industrial "villages" for the workforce.

Their experiments paved the way for

In Search of the Ideal City

modern city planning, which began with the work of Haussmann in Paris and Cerdà in Spain. Their innovative conception of the urban space as an administrative, economic, and cultural whole would progress by leaps and bounds during the twentieth century.

Noto Valley, Sicily, Italy. Eight towns in the valley were destroyed by the 1693 earthquake. Their reconstruction in the style of the Late Baroque denoted a new departure in urban architecture.
[Left-hand page] Modica.
[1] Noto.
[2] Villa Saraceno, Venetia, Italy; c. 1550.
By reinventing the architecture of Classical Rome, Andrea Palladio created a style that would inspire architects the world over.

[2] and [3]
Zamosc,
Poland.
An icon of the
Renaissance,
where the influ-
ence of Italian
architects inter-
acted with the
traditions of
central Europe.

[1] Úbeda.
[4] and [5] Baeza, Spain.
The renovation of these Andalusian towns helped introduce the Italian Renaissance to Spain in the early 16th century. Their design also served as a model for Latin America.

[1]–[3] and [Right-hand page] St. Petersburg, Russia. Founded in 1703 by Peter the Great, this former capital of the tsars emerged from a vast design project overseen by the leading architects of Europe. Its style is a mixture of baroque and neoclassicism.
[1] The Catherine Palace; 1751–1756.
[2] Chesma Cathedral; 1777–1780.
[3] Winter Palace; 1754–1762.
[Right-hand page] Church of the Resurrection of Christ; 1887–1907.

National Maritime Museum, Greenwich, England; 17th-18th centuries. The former Royal Naval College beside the Thames incorporates the earliest attempts at landscape architecture in the British Isles. At the center of a huge park based on designs by André Le Nôtre, the Queen's House of Inigo Jones was the nation's first Palladian construction. Christopher Wren added the remainder of the complex. In another innovative move, Wren sought the aid of scientist Robert Hooke for the design of the brick-built Royal Observatory, the first building specifically created for scientific purposes.

[Left-hand page]
Bath, England; 18th century.
A focal point of this ancient spa is the Circus, a circle of neoclassical town-houses grouped around what is now a roundabout, the work of urban architect John Wood.

[1] and [2] Place Stanislas, Nancy, France; 1752–1756.
Stanislas Leszczynski, the ousted king of Poland who became Duke of Lorraine, entrusted the architect Héré with an innovative urban project—a square that was both prestigious and functional.

The planet is bristling with fortresses that remind us how deeply humans have felt the need to protect themselves from danger and adversity. As both refuge and defense, the fortification is the armor of communities and peoples.

Throughout history, military architects have evolved ever more sophisticated responses to the threat of attack. Massive walls, keeps, towers, castles, fortified towns, strongholds, and bastions have been raised to resist attack both from humans and from time itself. In some cases, a vast and continuous defensive system guarded frontiers against invasion, like the Great Wall of China (4,188 miles/6,700 km) or the Roman limes (3,125 miles/5,000 km). In feudal Europe, local defenses were often centered on individual castles or villages, but these were formed into networks, just as in the Near East in the era of the Crusades.

Designers everywhere took advantage of the strategic possibilities offered by mountains or rivers and rendered their castles impregnable, even on the open plains.

Some have become legendary, such as the castles of Transylvania or the royal castle of Kronborg in Elsinore (Denmark), the setting of Shakespeare's *Hamlet*.

Other bastions occupy a vibrant place in the memory. Nearer to our own age, they stand as a universal symbol of the liberation

Formidable Fortresses

of the oppressed. Such are the citadel of Haiti, built by the first freed Negro slaves to protect the independence of their new republic, and Robben Island, a former South African penitentiary, emblematic of the resistance to apartheid and of the triumph of the human spirit over aggression.

[1]–[5] The Great Wall of China; 3rd century BC–Ming era (1368–1644). The world's largest defensive system extends for 4,188 miles (6,700 km) through 17 provinces in central and northern China. It was begun by Qin Shin Huang around 220 BC to link existing fortifications and establish a continuous frontier against invasion. Its construction played a major part in establishing the Empire.

[1] The Great Wall at Simatai.
[2] At Jinshanling.
[3] In Hebei Province.
[4] At Mutianyu.
[5] At Huang Hua Cheng.

[Following pages]
The Great Wall at Badaling.

[1] Bellinzona, Switzerland; 10th-15th century. The network of fortifications, based around three castles, protects the town and blocks the Tessin Valley.
[2] and [3] Ávila, Spain; 11th century. Built to guard against the Moors, the granite fortifications include 82 semicircular towers and 9 monumental gates.

Carcassonne, France; 4th to 13th century. The medieval city with its sturdy walls occupies a site fortified even before the Roman period. It was restored by Viollet-le-Duc in the mid-19th century, a major step forward in the conservation of historic monuments.

[1] Rhodes, Greece. Street of the Knights; fifteenth century. The upper town is the former stronghold of the Order of Hospitalers of St. John of Jerusalem (1309–1523).
[2] Spissky Hrad, Slovakia; 13th to 14th century. Part of Eastern Europe's largest medieval castle.

[3] Wartburg, Germany;
11th, 13th, and 19th
centuries.
This former castle was
also a breeding ground
of German culture.
[4] and [5] Sighisoara,
Romania; 19th century.
Sighisoara is a small
fortified town in
Transylvania founded by
a colony of artisans and
merchants from Saxony.

[1] and [2] Kazan Kremlin, Russia; 10th, 16th, and 19th centuries. Ivan the Terrible stormed the Tartar fortress in 1552 and made it the Christian capital of the lands around the Volga.
[3] Lahore fortress, Pakistan; 17th century. Its marble mosques and palaces bear testimony to the refinement of Moghul civilization.

[1] Red Fort, Agra, India; 17th century. The powerful Moghul citadel embraced the Imperial city and its extraordinary palaces.
[2] and [3] Himeji-jo, Japan; 1601–1609. Highly elaborate defensive systems surrounded this elegant castle, a remarkable example of timber construction.

349

Palace" derives from the Palatine Hill in Rome, where the emperors had their residence. We instantly associate the word with the dwelling of a powerful ruler and the court—and with a center of administration and power. Whether in the city or the country, it will be sumptuously appointed; a sublime instance of art at its most refined.

Many palaces are former castles that have been stripped of their defensive character while remaining vast monuments that both conserve and showcase the past. As usual in Western Europe, the Italian Renaissance set the fashion for new tastes, extending the accepted sense of a palace to pleasure villas and the grander private houses. Palatial architecture then developed a prestigious style based on a complex of spacious buildings, connecting courtyards, rows of columns and arcades, subtle ornamentation, and elaborate gardens and parks... Italian models and local traditions fused to inspire the greatest geniuses and most talented artists, from Fontainebleau to the Loire Valley, and in Moravia and Bohemia.

In the eighteenth century, Versailles became the model par excellence. Innumerable royal estates in Europe vied to equal it, and it developed a national style that soon spilled over into Romanticism.

In China, Japan, and Korea, the construction of imperial palaces, viewed as an art form for centuries, perpetuated the tradition of harmoniously integrating buildings into gardens perfectly adapted to the landscape of lakes, plains, and forests.

Jewel-like Palaces

Very different, the palaces of the powerful kings of Abomey were equally fascinating to the traveler who, within a single enclosure, was greeted by magnificent palaces of wood and earth raised to successive god-kings, rulers of the realms of both the living and the dead.

[1] and [3] Villa d'Este, Tivoli, Italy; 16th century. A fabulous ensemble of Italian Renaissance arts, the Villa d'Este combines architecture, landscaped gardens, and fountains. Its Italian gardens revolutionized landscaping practices in Europe.

[2], [4], and [5] Palace and park, Fontainebleau, France; 16th century. Francis I transformed the former fortress into a vast palace; inspired by the Italian Renaissance, it would play a major role in history of both the arts and the nation. Napoleon I refurbished it at the start of the 19th century.

[1]–[4] Chateaus of the Loire Valley, France. During the Renaissance, the Loire—the "royal river" of the Valois—became the focus of cultural and artistic exchanges between Italy, "la Doulce France," and Flanders. Francis I also built there, restoring Blois and launching the construction of Chambord. The landscaping techniques adopted in the region earned it the nickname "Garden of France."
[1] Saumur; 14th through 16th centuries.
[2] Blois; 13th through 15th and 17th centuries.

[3] Chenonceau;
16th century.
[4] Chambord; 16th
century.

[1]–[4] Palace and park of Versailles, France; 17th–18th century. The royal residence of Louis XIV became the model for classical French architecture, sculpture, furniture, landscaping, and painting.
[1] Le Grand Trianon (17th century) by Jules Hardouin-Mansart and Robert de Cotte.
[2] Hall of Mirrors (17th century) by architect François Mansart and painter Charles Le Brun.
[3] and [4] André Le Nôtre put the finishing touch to his masterpiece at Versailles with his "French gardens," copied by royal courts all over Europe.

[1] Palace of Westminster, London, England; 11th–19th century. The former royal residence was rebuilt in neo-Gothic style.
[2] Palace and gardens, Schönbrunn, Vienna, Austria; 18th century. The Imperial summer residence of the Habsburgs, in a form of baroque prefiguring Gesamtkunstwerk (multidisciplinary style).

[1] Palace and gardens of Sans-Souci, Potsdam, Germany; 1745. Rococo residence of Frederick II.
[2] Palace of DrottnIngholm, Sweden; 18th century. Private residence of the Swedish royal family. Both these buildings clearly illustrate the influence of Versailles in Europe.

[Left-hand page] Pena Palace, Sintra, Portugal; 1839. The eclectic palace and park of Ferdinand II ushered in the Romantic era of European architecture.
[1], [2], and [3] The Forbidden City (1406–1420) in Beijing, palace of the Ming and Qing dynasties, ranks as one of the foremost examples of Chinese imperial architecture.

361

The city is at once a center of political decision-making, the dynamic focus of economic activity, and a vibrant cultural forum where artistic ideas and currents flourish. The huge variety of building styles is clear evidence of this typically urban creativity.

Stimulated by their explosive growth, urban communities erected great buildings uniquely their own, beginning in medieval Europe with the city halls that were already winning the right to exercise local autonomy. In Northern France and Belgium, this process was reinforced by belfries rivaling and church steeples, tolling out the divisions of the working day.

The prosperity of the great cities gave rise to a monumental architecture designed to answer a variety of purposes: e.g., the Silk Exchange in Valencia (Spain), Victoria Station in Bombay, and the "Isle of Museums" in Berlin. Adversity imposed no less remarkable solutions, one of the finest being the Guadalajara Hospice (Mexico), a charitable institution as functional as it is aesthetic.

The effervescence of the human spirit found its expression in the urban landscape through the construction of cultural landmarks—the first printing and publishing houses in Antwerp, for instance. Equally, the visionary projects of the mid-nineteenth through twentieth centuries led to one

The Creative Impulse

aesthetic and conceptual revolution after another. Art Nouveau transfigured private houses and public buildings, while the use of reinforced concrete encouraged the modern international movement to make a clean sweep of architecture and adapt it to contemporary lifestyles.

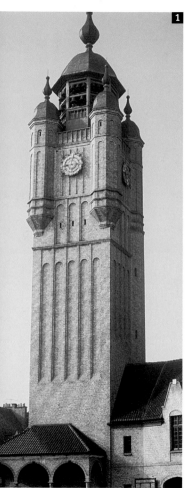

[1] Belfry, Bergues, France; 14th –16th century. Destroyed 1944, rebuilt 1961.
[2] *The Man of Fire* by José Clemente Orozco, 1938–9, Hospicio Cabañas, Guadalajara (19th–20th century), Mexico.
[3] Monticello, home of President Thomas Jefferson, Virginia, U.S.; 1769–1809.
[4] Chhatrapati Shivaji (formerly Victoria) Station, Bombay, India; 1878–1888.
A striking example of Victorian neo-Gothic in India.
[5] Independence Hall, Philadelphia, Pennsylvania, USA; 1732.
In this Georgian building, the Declaration of Independence (1776) and the Constitution of the United States (1787) were signed.

[1] Hotel van Eetvelde by Victor Horta, Brussels, Belgium; 1895.
Horta was one of the founders of Art Nouveau.
[2] The Rietveld Schröderhuis by Gerrit Thomas Rietveld, Utrecht, the Netherlands; 1924.
An icon of the De Stijl movement and modern architecture.

[3] and [4] Examples of the Bauhaus style, Dessau, Germany.
Constructed and decorated by professors at the Bauhaus, these buildings inaugurated the modernist movement in architecture.
[3] *Kornhaus* by Carl Fieger; 1929–30.
[4] *Meisterhaus* by Walter Gropius, c. 1925.

[Preceding pages] and [1]–[6] The architecture of Antoni Gaudí in Barcelona, Spain. Closely linked with Catalan Modernism, Naturalism, the Arts and Crafts Movement, and Art Nouveau, Gaudí's creative genius is expressed in a style that is simultaneously eclectic and personal, encompassing building techniques, architecture, landscape gardening, sculpture, and the decorative arts.

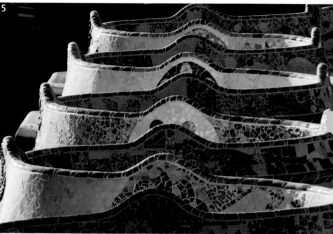

[Preceding pages] and [4] Casa Mila; 1906–1910.
[1] Casa Vicens; 1883–1888.
[2] Spires of the Sagrada Familia cathedral (Nativity façade); 1882–1926.
[3] and [6] Balconies and chimneys, Casa Batlló; 1904–1906.
[5] Serpentine bench, Güell Park; 1900–1914.

371

Wonderful Cultural Landscapes

The continents are crisscrossed by ancient trading routes and the corridors pierced by conquering races. Like bonds stretched between peoples and civilizations, they have linked the whole world in an amazing network of exchanges and encounters. At every point, the blend of cultures is unique.

Ancient ways like the legendary incense, spice, and gold routes once traversed every land, ignoring frontiers and crossing deserts, mountains, and rivers to link East and West, North and South. Where routes met or on newly created sites, men built resting places for their caravans; these became ideal locations for cultural exchange—oases of ideas and cultural wealth where traditions were thrown into the melting-pot. They bear magical names like Bukhara and Samarkand in Uzbekistan, Bam (Iran), Aleppo and Bosra (Syria), Safranbolu (Turkey), Chinguetti (Mauritania), Marrakesh (on the threshold of the Moroccan desert), and Lijiang in China.

Successive changes in the balance of power in strategic areas also gave rise to a cultural heritage that was diverse, yet harmonious, and constantly being renewed. Sicily, for instance, is home to cultures developed over 3,000 years in the Mediterranean region and Europe. Spain, under Moorish domination, invented the mudejar art of Aragon and particularly the dazzling Arab-Andalusian culture that saw Cordoba rival Constantinople, Damascus, and Baghdad and which re-emerged triumphantly in Morocco.

One city, Mostar (Bosnia-Hertzegovina), has become a universal symbol in our era;

The Crossroads of Civilization

ravaged by war, it is, thanks to faithful reconstruction, winning back its former image, acquired through centuries of peaceful coexistence between different communities.

[1] Lviv, Ukraine.
A frontier city long shared between Austria and Poland, Lviv remains imprinted with the traditions of its earlier communities.
[2] Naples, Italy.
The city enshrines 25 centuries of Mediterranean culture. Here, the 13th-century cloisters of San Martino.

[1] and [2] Syracuse, Sicily, Italy. A city successively shaped by the Greeks, Romans, Byzantines, Arabs, Normans, Frederick II of Hohenstaufen, the Spanish Aragon, and Bourbon dynasties... and 3,000 years of Mediterranean civilization.
[1] The Greek theater.
[2] The Roman amphitheater.

[1] Cáceres, Spain.
From Moorish towers to Roman, Gothic, and Renaissance buildings, the juxtaposition of styles recalls the city's turbulent past.
[2] and [3] Salamanca, Spain.
Carthaginians, Romans, and Moors ruled this city in turn. It gained its well-known university in the Middle Ages.
[2] The university.
[3] Plaza Mayor.
[4] Alcázar, Toledo, Spain.
The heritage of Toledo owes much to a variety of religions, in particular Judaism, Christianity, and Islam.

4

5

Andalusia, Spain, is the repository of rare and outstanding relics of medieval Arab culture.

[1] and [2] Seville cathedral. The bell tower, or Giralda, was once a minaret   a remarkable example of Almohad architecture (12th century). The 15th/16th-century cathedral, containing the tomb of Christopher Columbus, is Spain's largest Gothic structure. [Right-hand page] The Alhambra (fortress-palace), Grenada; 14th century.

[1] Medina of Tetuan, Morocco. A point of contact between Morocco and Andalusia.
[2] The ramparts of Marrakesh, Morocco. From its position on the edge of the desert, the capital of the Almoravids (1056–1147) ruled North Africa and Andalusia.

[1] and [2] Meknes, Morocco.
After welcoming refugees from Andalusia in the 13th century, including a Jewish community, Meknes became the capital of Moulay Ismaïl (1672–1727). The sultan was fascinated by Europe and rebuilt Meknes in a medley of Spanish and Moorish styles.
[1] Bab Mansour el Aleuj gate.
[2] Mausoleum of Sultan Moulay Ismaïl.

385

Oases and caravan cities of central Asia.
[1] Bukhara, Uzbekistan; Kalyan mosque; 16th century.
[2] Samarkand, Uzbekistan; Bibi-Khanum mosque; early 15th century.
[3] Ichan Kala, Khiva, Uzbekistan.
[Right-hand page] Bam, Iran (before the 2003 earthquake).

Liberty Lighting the World by
Frédéric-Auguste Bartholdi
(1886)
New York, Atlantic Ocean, U.S.

The Phoenicians established the first ports around the Mediterranean. Thereafter, new maritime routes were continuously developed, and thriving ports sprang up on every coast, gateways for trade and the movement of peoples around the seven seas. Some became the nuclei for trading empires.

The construction of ports went hand in hand with the remarkable progress of seaborne exchanges. Venice—La Serenissima—became the gateway to the Orient; hers was the dominant economy of Europe and her cultural flowering still dazzles us today. In northern Europe, dozens of cities joined the Hanseatic League, the commercial empire of the North Sea and the Baltic. Oman was another magnet for trade, as was Lamu (Kenya) on the Indian Ocean, where Arab, Persian, Indian, and European influences jostled with Swahili culture... From the earliest times, ports were incorporated into systems of coastal defense and saw out the centuries safely behind fortifications and beneath the watchful gaze of a citadel.

This was the model exported by Portugal, Spain, and other European powers to the New World, Africa, Asia, and the islands that served as staging posts.

The colonial heritage of the port cities with their kaleidoscopic cultural mix and memories of the great explorations includes evidence of the slave trade. We cannot but remember, for instance, that the fortress of Brimstone Hill in the Caribbean was designed by the British, but constructed by African slaves. On the other hand, the Aapravasi Ghat in Mauritius—a

Cities Beside the Sea

transit zone for free workers en route from India—symbolizes the start of modern migrations... And at the entrance to the port of New York stands the Statue of Liberty, presented by the French nation; a sight that has greeted millions of immigrants.

[1]–[4] Venice, Adriatic Sea, Italy. Known as La Serenissima, the gateway of the West to the Orient was already a maritime power in the tenth century. The city is built on a lagoon; there are 118 small islands and 200 canals connected by 400 bridges...

.... For its architecture alone, Venice would be a wonder of the world, its palaces and churches showcases for priceless works of art.
[1] Canal in the San Marco quarter.
[2] Piazza San Marco (St. Mark's Square), the heart of the city.

[3] Chiesa di San Giorgio Maggiore by Andrea Palladio; 1566–1580.
[4] The Grand Canal.

[1] El-Jazar mosque (1781), the Old Town, Acre, Mediterranean Sea, Israel.
The Crusaders' capital became a typical Ottoman city port.
[2] Liverpool, Mersey estuary, England; 18th to 20th centuries.
A major center of world trade and port of embarkation for countless migrants to America
[3] Dubrovnik, Adriatic Sea, Croatia.
The "Pearl of the Adriatic" was once a major sea power.

[1] Essaouira (formerly Mogador), Atlantic Ocean, Morocco.
The city was founded in 1765 on the site of an old Portuguese fortress. The sultan entrusted the project to a French military engineer.
[2] Willemstad, island of Curaçao, Dutch Antilles, Caribbean Sea, the Netherlands.
A Dutch commercial station established in 1634 to trade with the Portuguese and Spanish colonies.

[1]–[4] Cities of the Hanseatic League, the medieval trading empire of northern Europe.
[1] and [2] Bryggen, the old wharf of Bergen on the Vägen Fjord, Norway.
[3] and [4] Visby, Gotland Island, Baltic Sea, Sweden.
[Right-hand page] Karlskrona, Baltic Sea, Sweden; late eighteenth century.
A purpose-built naval port.

Angra do Heroismo, Terceira Island, Azores archipelago, Atlantic Ocean, Portugal. The port, necessarily fortified, was an obligatory stopping place on the main sea routes from the fifteenth century until the appearance of steam vessels in the 1800s.

[1] and [2] Porto, Douro estuary, Atlantic Ocean, Portugal.
Founded by the Romans, it was the capital of the country until the twelfth century. It continues to prosper, thanks to the wine trade.
[1] The Ribeira, historic center of Porto.
[2] Cloister of the Sé, or cathedral, its walls incrusted with azulejos.

397

[1] and [2] Island of Gorée, Atlantic Ocean, Senegal.
The foremost center of the slave trade.
[1] The Slave House.
[3] Carthagena, Caribbean Sea, Colombia.
Fortified port founded by the Spaniard Don Pedro de Herredia in 1533.
[4] Valparaiso, Pacific Ocean, Chile.
Another Spanish foundation (1544).

[1] Fort St. Catherine, St. George's Island, Bermuda, Atlantic Ocean, UK. One of the earliest British settlements in the New World.

[2] Brimstone Hill fortress, St. Kitts, Antilles, Caribbean Sea, St. Kitts and Nevis. A triumph of seventeenth- and eighteenth-century British military engineering, constructed with the labor of African slaves.

Olinda, founded in the
sixteenth century by the
Portuguese in Brazil

The gradual extension of Europe's influence in the world from the late fifteenth century, including the establishment of the Portuguese, Spanish, and later French, British, and Dutch colonial empires, led to the development, over the course of three centuries, of extremely varied and eclectic forms of art and urban design.

Colonial art first appeared, through necessity, in the field of architecture. Between the sixteenth and nineteenth centuries, Spain and Portugal, which controlled the greater part of the Americas, created a whole network of new towns and cities to administer and convert their empires. The Spanish adopted for their colonies a rigorous system of city planning based on the checkerboard design. Constructed on the remains of pre-Columbian civilizations (e.g., Cuzco) or from scratch (Puebla, Antigua), colonial towns were organized around a "civic center," or main square bordered by arcades, where the principal church stood side by side with the governor's mansion. A similar layout was imposed on native villages set up around Franciscan, Dominican, and Augustinian monasteries—the "missions"—and subsequently in the Jesuit "Reductions."

Planners had to adapt to the terrain, the risk of earthquakes, and the local climate by borrowing from indigenous traditions. The varied styles imported by architects or master masons trained in Europe were reinterpreted by native or mixed-race workers; buildings thus acquired a heteroclite style

Foundations of the New World

that led to the decorative exuberance and abundant polychromy of colonial baroque. In those areas that prospered from exploiting silver or gold deposits, such as Zacatecas or Ouro Preto, the native vitality and power of expression far surpassed the most prolific European models.

[1] Cholula, Mexico, conquered in the sixteenth century by the Spanish. The church of Nuestra Señora de los Remedios (eighteenth century) was constructed on top of a pyramid, at the foot of Popocatépetl.
[2] and [3] Old Lunenburg, Nova Scotia, Canada.
A British colony (1753) built entirely of timber.

Querétaro, Mexico; sixteenth-
century Spanish colony.
From the start, the European
quarter, built to a geometric
design, coexisted alongside the
maze of alleys housing the
indigenous Otomi, Tarasco, and
Chichimeca peoples. Here, the
seventeenth-century monastery
of Santa Cruz.

[1] Oaxaca, Mexico, founded in the 1500s by the Spanish and constructed by Dominicans.
The city lies close to the pre-Hispanic site of Monte Albán.
The monastery of Santo Domingo.
[2] Morelia, Mexico, also founded in the sixteenth century by Spain, is built on a geometric plan modified by the demands of the terrain.
The cathedral.

Puebla, Mexico, built on an empty site by the Spanish in 1531. A prosperous colonial city at the foot of Popocatépetl, Puebla swarmed with churches and sumptuous mansions in a fusion of styles. The azulejos incrusting the walls are particularly noteworthy.

[1]

[2]

[1] Trinidad, Cuba.
Spanish foundation of
1514 and bridgehead
for the conquest of the
continent.
[2] Antigua Guatemala,
former capital of
Guatemala, founded by
Spain in 1543.
[Right-hand page]
Cienfuegos, Cuba,
founded in 1819 by a
Frenchman from
Bordeaux under the
tutelage of the
Spanish.

[1] Arequipa, Peru, founded by Spain; 1540. Its architecture is a blend of Spanish and local techniques. Santa Catalina monastery.
[2] Ouro Preto, Brazil, founded by gold hunters at the end of the 17th century. The work of the baroque sculptor Aleijadinho highlights the city's prosperous past.

[1] Santa Ana de los Ríos de Cuenca, Ecuador, founded by the Spanish in 1557. A colonial city of the interior, among the valleys of the Andes.
[2] Cuzco, the Andes, Peru, conquered in 1536 by Spain. Baroque churches and palaces now throng the site of the former Inca capital. The cathedral.

Cultural Landscapes, Cultivated Landscapes

The concept of the "cultural landscape" was defined by the World Heritage Convention in 1992. Since then, numerous sites categorized as "the combined work of mankind and nature" have been added to the World Heritage List.

Cultural landscapes express "a longstanding and intimate relationship between peoples and their environment." Whether the result of maximizing the value of the land and exploiting natural resources, or of an association with religious or artistic practices, they have been, so to speak, "humanized" and consequently closely linked to the identity of society and mankind as a whole.

Many of these sites illustrate the labors expended over time to render a location habitable, especially if of strategic value. Some reveal traces of human activity long ceased, such as St. Kilda in the Hebrides, deserted after two thousand years of occupation. Others remain the living and rare conservatories of traditional knowledge vital for the maintenance of biological diversity. From the agropastoral system of the Pyrenees to world-famous vineyards, from Cuban valley plantations to Mexican landscapes of agaves and tequila distilleries, mankind has joined forces with nature to make the most of the accidents of geography—good and bad—in harmonious partnership.

There are cultural landscapes governed by the principles of good management, like the Orcia Valley (Italy), or by sacred traditions, such as the purpose-designed landscapes of Champassak (Laos), the mountains of Wudang (China), and the terraced rice fields of the Philippines... or again the domesticated plateau of Sukur (Nigeria), where social life revolves around the palace of the spiritual and temporal chief, the Hidi.

Archipelago of St. Kilda, Western Hebrides, Scotland, United Kingdom.
The last inhabitants departed in 1930 after two thousand years of human occupation, abandoning the spectacular volcanic landscape to wild creatures and the ruins of the sheep farms.

Ibiza, Spain. The coasts and waters around Ibiza enjoy a rich biodiversity, while the island's long history has molded its cultural landscape. Here, traces of the ancient Phoenician colony survive under the watchful eye of the Renaissance Catalan citadel, which incorporates the former Arab medina.

[1]⊢[3]
Portovenere and the Cinque Terre, Liguria, Italy. Long inaccessible by land, the rugged cliffs were both an obstacle and a defensive barrier. The inhabitants established themselves only by creating terraces and anchoring their homes to the rock.
[1] Manarola
[2] Portovenere
[3] Corniglia

[1] and [2] Coast of Amalfi, Italy.
Man has occupied this magnificent shoreline since the early Middle Ages, developing it by establishing terrace cultures, vineyards, and orchards. This is necessarily a densely built environment with buildings stacked up the cliff sides, but many are of exceptional architectural merit.
[1] Amalfi
[2] Ravello

Terraced rice fields in Ifugao province, the Philippines. These high-altitude terraces have been redrawing the contours of the cordilleras for two thousand years. The harmonious curves of the terracing combine ancestral wisdom and sacred tradition to ensure the balance of the community.

Viñales Valley, Cuba.
Scooped from the awesomely rugged limestone terrain, the valley is a living landscape thriving on tobacco growing. The
villagers carry on age-old peasant traditions and agricultural practices although
the valley's well-known folk music draws
on a variety of sources.

[1] and [2] Agave fields near the volcanic Mt. Tequila, Mexico. Cultivation of the blue or tequila agave on an industrial scale has given rise to these vast expanses. Familiar even to the pre-Hispanic inhabitants, the plant, which is almost unique to the area, has become synonymous with Mexico.

[3] Orcia Valley, Tuscany. An agricultural landscape colonized according to the criteria of the Italian Renaissance—the preservation of beauty, and good management.

Charterhouse of San Lorenzo di Padula, Vallo di Diano, Italy. The Cilento and Vallo di Diano National Park is an exceptional cultural landscape, while the mountains form a line of communication between the Adriatic and the Tyrrhenian Sea, exploited by successive civilizations for over two millennia.

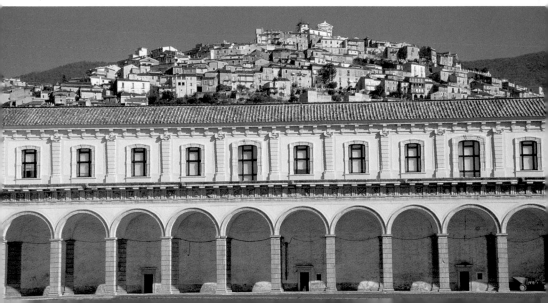

Vineyard landscapes. The vine is an accepted symbol of civilization; first planted systematically by the Romans, it tamed the land and dictated the organization of villages and trade.
[1] Tokaj, Hungary
[2] Upper Douro, Portugal
[3] Juridiction de Saint-Émilion, France

[4] Hallstatt, Salzkammergut, Austria. This area, renowned for the splendor of its natural landscape and its scientific and historical associations, was the site of a Celtic Iron Age society that exploited the salt deposits from c. 2,000 BC—the Hallstatt civilization.

Ait-Ben-Haddou, Morocco.
A ksar, or fortified earthen
village, in the pre-Saharan
region

If there is a universal phenomenon that signals the presence of humanity on the face of the Earth, it must be the house. The ancestral dwelling, the remarkable result of human capacity to adapt to the environment, is imprinted with a complete record of social and cultural traditions.

Square, rectangular, round, or just a cave, and with pointed, sloping, or plain flat roofs, the design of traditional housing depends upon local geography, climate, available materials, and the technological possibilities offered by nature.

Consequently, villages built of wood, earth, vegetable matter, or stone often seem to melt into the landscape. In such places, humans reveal their amazing skill in protecting themselves from heat or cold, damp, rain and snow, judiciously combining the choice of materials with decisions about orientation, the arrangement of doors and windows, and the ideal slope of the roof for storm-water drainage.

These homes form a living heritage for their occupants; they, or the community, are their own architects. On a single site we find a wide range of individual solutions employed by distinct cultural groups. For the plan of the traditional dwelling is not dictated solely by necessity; it is an organized space, closely associated with lifestyle, governing the community.

A Place Called Home

The traditional house encapsulates a symbolic representation of how a culture views the family structure, relations between the sexes, and social organization in general.

For all these reasons, it is essential that such communities be preserved.

[1] and [2] Gassho houses in the high mountains of Chubu, Honshu, Japan.
The inhabitants of these isolated villages have developed a quite unique form of farmhouse suited to their occupation (breeding silk worms) and their environment.
[1] Village of Ogimachi.
[2] Village of Shirakawa-go.
[Right-hand page] Tower houses in Mestia, Upper Svaneti, Caucasus, Georgia.
The medieval tower-house fulfilled the dual purpose of dwelling and defense against invasion.

[3] Hongcun, Anhui province, China.
In this traditional Chinese village, the water supply was organized by a geomancer.

The trulli of Alberobello, Apulia, Italy.
These groups of dwellings are constructed using a technique inherited from prehistory—drystone, i.e., without mortar. This was the villagers' simplest response to local conditions, as limestone slabs could be gathered from neighboring fields...

... and all that was necessary was to build the houses directly on the rock. At Alberobello, the trulli are typically rectangular with conical roofs, but the latter may also be pyramid or dome shaped.

[1]–[4] and [Following pages] Trogdolyte villages in the Göreme Valley, Cappadocia, Turkey. Cappadocia is a kind of natural citadel with a labyrinth of caves and passages hollowed out of the tufa by erosion. Christians who took refuge there from the fourth century began to add dwellings, sheepfolds, pigeon houses, underground towns, and even churches, which they covered with Byzantine paintings in the post-Iconoclast style. The Christians were forced out in 1923 and the last inhabitants deserted the valley a few decades later.

Models of traditional urban design

[1] Djenné, on the banks of the Niger, Mali. The banco houses are raised on mounds as a precaution against flooding.
[2] and [3] Taos, Rio Grande Valley, New Mexico, U.S.. Adobe architecture has a thousand-year-old history and was inherited from the Pueblo Indians.

Muslim townships were often isolated, with each community based on family structure. [1] Ghardaia and ksour (fortified villages) of the M'Zab Valley, Algeria. Their harmony is a source of inspiration for planners. [2] Shibam, Yemen. The "Manhattan of the desert" with earthen buildings set against a backdrop of sheer cliffs.

Controlling the water supply, preparing the soil, selecting plants, "... this is an art / Which does mend nature, change it rather—but / The art itself is Nature." (Shakespeare, *The Winter's Tale*). In other words, human genius adds its contribution to creation to organize the way we live...

That human beings have turned the art of irrigation and drainage into a science is clear from the worldwide network of waterways, some of which have served entire regions for thousands of years. Arid terrains rely on the life-giving water of oases and, from Oman to the palm groves of Elche (Spain)—a unique instance of Arab agricultural practices imported to Europe—the distribution of this precious resource is the determining factor in social and economic organization.

Equally ingenious are the technologies adopted by hydraulic engineers in areas where the abundance of water imposes a need for flood defenses, as in the Low Countries and around the Min Jiang River (China). Networks of canals and polders—land that has been drained and reclaimed—have also created new landscapes often boasting impressive industrial complexes.

Water, naturally, has a special place in gardens and parks. Indeed, the very first botanical garden, founded in Padua in 1545, was designed as a representation of Paradise and surrounded by a ribbon of water. From a different metaphysical perspective, the finest Chinese man-made landscapes excel in recreating or integrating every kind of natural scenery.

The Earth as Garden

Canals and lakes are also highlights of the wonderful Moghul gardens of Shalimar (Pakistan) and of all those designs that were models for Europe, like those of classical France, the landscaped parks of the Age of Enlightenment, or the English Romantic garden ...

The Royal Botanic Gardens, Kew, London, England. Since its creation in 1759, Kew has housed collections intimately linked with the scientific study of plants...

436

... and with ecology. The historic landscaped garden is the setting for buildings and plant houses—notably the Temperate House—that epitomize Victorian glass and cast-iron architecture.

[1]–[5] Chinese landscaped gardens.
In China, landscaping is both an art and a philosophy—a metaphysical representation of natural beauty. The traditional urban structure as developed by Chinese civilization exists in sympathy with the environment, fashioning it with meticulous care and incorporating hills, water, vegetation, and architecture to create a setting where beauty reigns amid peace and harmony.
[1]–[3] The classical gardens of Suzhou; 11th–19th century.
[4] and [5] The Imperial Garden, Summer Palace, Beijing; 18th–19th century.

Shalimar Gardens, Lahore, Pakistan; 17th century. The crowning glory of Moghul civilization. Overflowing with plants and flowers, as refined as they are huge, the gardens are laid out in the form of three successive terraces and include pavilions, waterfalls, and lakes.

Garden Kingdom of Dessau-Wörlitz,
Germany; 18th century.
This archetypal landscape of the Age of
Enlightenment, consisting of parks, English-style
gardens, agricultural land, and urban structures,
demonstrates how aesthetics were enlisted in the
service of progress and science.

[1]–[5] Canal du Midi, France; 1667–1681. Its 150 miles (240 km) of navigable water link the Mediterranean to the Atlantic, while its 328 structures (locks, aqueducts, bridges, spillways, and tunnels) make it a formidable example of modern civil engineering. Its advanced technology foreshadowed the Industrial Revolution...

... while its architectural qualities and deliberate landscaping ensure it is also a work of art.
[1] Puichéric, Aude.
[2] Argeliers, Aude.
[3] and [5] Toulouse, Haute-Garonne.
[4] Capestang, Hérault.

[1]–[3] Water drainage and land reclamation, Schokland, the Netherlands. Remains of churches, terps (mounds on which villages were built), and Stone Age archeological deposits reveal that this former region of peat bogs was inhabited from ancient times. Eventually overwhelmed by the sea, the area had to be evacuated in 1859. The drainage of the Zuiderzee in 1940 permitted its reclamation, creating a brand-new landscape.

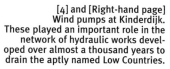

[4] and [Right-hand page] Wind pumps at Kinderdijk. These played an important role in the network of hydraulic works developed over almost a thousand years to drain the aptly named Low Countries.

Many countries owe their present-day structure to the previous two centuries of industrial and technical development. In the third millennium, however, faced with economic globalization and new technologies, our industrial panoply, once the witness of intense and innovative activity, has become a legacy of the past and the stuff of memory.

The deindustrialization of the West has left the remains of a technology that was once the last word in productiveness, but is now under threat or obsolete. This legacy enshrines a vast amount of human history and technical skill. The unique architecture of factories and manufacturing plants was adapted to methods of production; just as typically, however, it conformed to the tastes and ideologies of the owners, bypassing aesthetic considerations to embrace the identity of an era marked by economic, social, and technical revolution. Similarly, machines and tools, the material traces of the scientific prowess and high technology of the nineteenth and twentieth centuries, preserve the memory of the massive mechanization of labor.

The enormous scope of the industrial era can be gauged equally well from our urban fabric, the mountain railroads of Austria or India, or structures as diverse as the Vizcaya ferry bridge in Bilbao (Spain) and the transatlantic radio station at Varberg (Sweden). The environment, in fact, remains indelibly imprinted by industrial installations. Mining landscapes, fashioned

Our Industrial Heritage

by the exploitation of mineral or coal deposits, are spectacular examples of this, some of them extremely old, like the former gold mines of Las Médulas (Spain), the model medieval mines at Banská Stiavnica (Slovakia), and Wieliczka (Poland), source of rock salt for over seven centuries.

The mining city of Roros, Norway.
Roros was founded in the seventeenth century to exploit the newly discovered copper deposits. Its regular layout indicates it was adapted to the demands of the mountainous site and the mine, while its timber buildings are in the local architectural tradition. The existence of both a workers' village and houses grouped around farmyards, however, is proof that the inhabitants pursued more than one activity. Copper was mined for 333 years, until 1977.

[1] The Iron Bridge, Ironbridge Gorge, Shropshire, England; 1773. The world's first cast-iron bridge was built to serve the blast furnace at Coalbrookdale, scene of the earliest experiments with coke smelting.
[2] and [3] Goslar, Germany. The medieval city owed its prosperity to the Rammelsberg mines and their rich seams of silver and metallic ores. Goslar was a member of the Hanseatic League.
[2] Chamber of Homage, Town Hall; c. 1500.

[4] and [5] Guanajuato, Mexico. Founded by the Spanish in the early 1600s, by the 18th century the city had become the world's most important center for the extraction of silver.

Potosí, Bolivia. Perched over 13,100 ft (4,000 m) in the Bolivian Andes, Potosí was founded in 1546 at the foot of the Cerro Rico ("rich mountain"), reputed to contain the world's biggest silver ore deposits...

... Some 5,000 exploitations took place in the mining city up to the early nineteenth century, resulting in the creation of a large network of aqueducts and lakes to provide waterpower for the crushing mills. The colonial city's grand array of churches and baroque palaces contrasts with the barrios mitayos, or workers' quarters.

The Royal Salt Works, Arc-et-Senans,
France; 1775–1779.
The work of architect Claude Nicolas Ledoux,
the plant was the first large-scale example of
industrial design, laid out in the form of a
semicircle in accordance with contemporary
principles that organized production in
rational, hierarchical, and social terms...

... dictating the organization of work in that epoch. Originating in the reign of Louis XVI, the salt works are steeped in the ethos of progress so beloved of the Age of Enlightenment. The initial project also foresaw the addition of an "ideal" industrial city, which was never realized. The complex was abandoned in 1890.

[1]–[3] and [Right-hand page] Mountain railroads in India were based on technology exported to their colonies by the British. Employing audacious technical solutions, they constructed lines for travelers to access previously isolated mountain regions.
[1] and [3] Nilgiri Mountain Railway, Tamil Nadu; 1891–1908.
[2] and [Right-hand page] Darjeeling Himalayan Railway, West Bengal; 1881.

Index of locations

Photo Credits

All the photos in this book were provided by Agence Corbis.

Other titles in the 1001 Photos collection:
Football
Rugby
Horses
Baby Animals
Dogs
Cats
Airplanes
Trains
Dream Cars
Egypt
Farm Animals
Flowers